With love,
Melissa Hekkers

Amir's Blue Elephant

Armida Publications is a member of the
Independent Publishers Guild (UK),
and a member of the Independent Book Publishers Association (USA)

www.armidabooks.com | Great Literature. One Book At A Time.

Summary:
Melissa Hekkers recounts her footsteps as she joins the
journey of thousands of refugees seeking safety in Europe.

Pushing the boundaries of creative non-fiction, Hekkers recreates the moments that marked her the most, whilst volunteering in refugee camps in Lesvos, Greece, and during her ongoing involvement with the refugee community in Cyprus.

Amir's Blue Elephant is a glimpse into the sorrows of one of the biggest challenges faced by humanity today. Told through the eyes of a woman struggling to understand the realities asylum seekers are thrown into, this is the story of people fighting for the fragile right to freedom and liberty, the right to life itself.

[1. SOCIAL SCIENCE / Emigration & Immigration, 2. SOCIAL SCIENCE / Refugees,
3. SOCIAL SCIENCE / Volunteer Work, 4. SOCIAL SCIENCE / Human Geography,
5. SOCIAL SCIENCE / Social Classes & Economic Disparity,
6. BIOGRAPHY & AUTOBIOGRAPHY / Social Activists, 7. BIOGRAPHY & AUTOBIOGRAPHY / Women,
8. BIOGRAPHY & AUTOBIOGRAPHY /Editors, Journalists, Publishers]

Cover
Photo by Orlova Maria on Unsplash
Photo by Keyur Nandaniya on Unsplash

This memoir is a truthful recollection of actual events in the author's life.
Some conversations have been recreated and/or supplemented.
The names and details of some individuals have been changed to respect their privacy.

1st edition: September 2020

ISBN-13 (paperback): 978-9925-573-31-8

MELISSA HEKKERS

Amir's Blue Elephant

A WOMAN'S JOURNEY INTO THE LIVES OF EUROPE'S REFUGEES

ARMIDA

Table of Contents

Acknowledgements

The journey that led me to write this book is very close to my heart. It's through the realms of a humanitarian crisis that I met myself. It's also where I met hundreds of people who cultivated my passion for humanity, for righteousness and for a way of life that meets eye-to-eye with my virtues and visions. It can only be symbolic to want to thank each of these people. Yet there are specific people who have contributed to making this book a reality, and this is why I want to single them out here. The Casale Flaminia Residency, Ralph Overbeck in particular and Mellisa Felix, my mentor, for your support, encouragement, trust and abundant guidance. My Publisher (Armida Books), Haris Ioannides, for embracing my work and pushing on through, my parents and family for an ever growing faith in my never ending (ad)ventures, my closest of friends -you know who you are- who insistently remind me that following your dreams is non-negotiable and my daughter, for all her brightness.

For Lara

Chapter 1

Breaking Free

My work desk was neat and tidy. Like it was every morning. The only remains of last night's shift was my empty coffee cup. The lingering brown coffee grounds at the bottom of the cup resembled the way I felt. Dry. Stagnant. Empty. Not much to say for myself; unless someone was willing to read my coffee cup; delve into its whispers. I guess that would be a solution to finding my way around my next steps. Let someone else envision my life for a while. Day in, day out, the gloom of the newsroom impelled me to break loose; forget about everything and seek the truth elsewhere than within the news headlines.

As a journalist, I had been preoccupied with the ever-growing refugee crisis for the past ten years, at the very least, although it somehow felt like much longer than that. By nature I felt that I had been a migrant all my life. I had migrated from my birth country with my mother at the age of eight and I had never really acquired a new home; or the feeling of belonging that I imagined was attached to it. This was one of the reasons why my career as a journalist very much revolved around migration issues. It spoke to me.

Yet at the peak of the crisis in 2015, I felt that my purpose to divulge the truth about what really lay behind the movement of peoples wasn't being met. I was done with reporting on the number of boats that crossed the shores of Turkey and Libya into Italy and Greece. I wasn't interested in the battles NGOs fought with local authorities on the ways the influx of people was being (mal) handled. I was weary of government spiels on the immensity of the problem. And I was silently witnessing the urgent needs of people being uprooted from the destinies they had worked on for an entire lifetime to realise. Just like thousands of us around the world, I was guilty of assessing their truth based on assumption.

"So what you working on today?" blurted Oliver, my editor-in-chief, a tall, middle-aged man who carried himself well and whose grey goatee defined his composure. Over the years, he had defiantly managed to keep me on my toes and in consequence I repeatedly second-guessed the actuality I purveyed through my words. Deep down, his judgement centred on an ambiguity I knew wasn't justified yet his position of power allowed it. Rarely did he accept any piece of my writing without having something to add, something to nitpick.

"Is this geezer real?" he asked me, pointing at one of the stories I had written for the morning paper. He was scanning the newspaper as he paced around the office. As I watched him prance around, he stretched his arm out to switch the radio on.

"Those were his words Oliver. Word for word," I replied as a matter of fact. My tone of voice indicated that I had no time for his whims. I had written a story about a family of stateless Syrian Kurds who were on a hunger strike outside the presidential palace, seeking Cypriot nationality and consequently freedom of movement. I despised the way he dismissed people's opinions, their aspirations, and merely anything that wasn't logically sound. He disregarded any piece of writing that had a human angle to it. He wanted numbers. He wanted facts. He wanted the cold reality.

"But do you believe him, is the question," he added speaking slower than usual with the irritating smirk he so often made use of. He was an avid football fan who brought his four sons up with a vengeance. He thrived on asking rhetorical questions that shattered my approach to news writing, yet throughout the years I had always maintained that what true journalism was really about was discovering the truth and more importantly letting others tell the story, unfiltered through my own biases and understandings.

The sound of the fax machine behind us jolted me back to Oliver's question. As if he'd never left the '90s, he still relied on these relics. The fax machine should have been something of the distant past yet he lived by it; at times I joked that press releases printed on fax paper descended from another era. But before I managed to formulate a full sentence in response, he had already scanned the fax he had just picked up from the fax machine and threw it on my desk like a Frisbee.

"Here's a story. Two English Typhoon jets are being

deployed from the RAF's base in Limassol to back the military action against the so-called Islamic State in Syria. Write something about that. For the website. It must be up on Reuters already."

"Jesus," I muttered to myself as I scanned the document. I had just booked a one-way ticket to the Greek island of Lesvos[1] to get a closer look at what the refugee crisis looked like on the ground. On the one hand, I wanted to get a concrete understanding of what Syrian people were fleeing from, what their take on the war was, what they were enduring but, more importantly perhaps, I was seeking to stand by them on their journeys. I wanted to tell them that I intrinsically understood what it meant to 'lose' your home, how it felt to have to deal with migration bureaucratic whims and what was implied when you found yourself in a position where your mother tongue has no power and in a place where your means are totally insufficient to build the life you hope for.

"All I need is jet planes flying along with me," I continued to mutter to myself as I reread the facsimile.

I swirled around on my chair in an attempt to get up to go and fill my coffee cup with some substance. As I stepped forward, lifting myself off my chair, I accidently pulled the Internet connection wire out of its socket. Nothing was easy or perhaps this was the beginning of another underlying story that would define my day. I bent over and knelt down to reconnect the wire just as I heard Oliver re-enter the room.

---

[1] Lesvos (also called Lesbos or Mytilini).

"Need any help there love? It's a bit early to be on all fours, no?" he sniffed.

My blood pressure hit the roof but, closing my eyes tightly shut, I forced myself to remain steady. Once I had made my way out from under my desk and perhaps plucked enough courage to speak my mind, Oliver had disappeared.

I patted the dust I had collected from under the desk from my knees, I lifted my coffee cup off the desktop and headed for the door. I knew it was going to be a long day.

Chapter 2

The Departure

From the day I booked my ticket I had doubts about my choice. Admittedly, I was taking a break from the newsroom I so resented. In many ways I think I believed I could change the world by seeking and acknowledging its cruelty. But in truth, as a single mother, I was leaving my 8-year-old little girl behind in order to attend to other people's needs.

Dara was young, bold and as clumsy as I was. Light in her being but hefty in her will, she never ceased to surprise me.

"Mom, you know my blue elephant? The teddy I won at that festival we went to in the mountains?" she called out from her bedroom as I meticulously packed the last bits and pieces I envisaged I may need.

I shuffled around in contemplation, holding a flash light in my right hand and a map of Lesvos I had insisted on taking with me in the other. As if a paper map would guide my way and not the calamity of Lesvos' plight.

"Euh, I think so... You mean the one with the chequered bib? I think it's on your bed." Dara was forever losing things; she depended somewhat on my photographic memory to find her own belongings.

"I know it's on my bed mom, it's here," she appeared in my bedroom holding the blue teddy in her hands, waving it from side-to-side, confirming that she could find things if she really put her mind to it. I was about to comment but opted to remain silent. I was leaving tomorrow after all; better not stir things.

"Take it with you," she said, throwing it on top of my rucksack. "Give it to someone there. A refugee. I don't need it. I have exactly the same one, the one that Zara gave to me. Remember? I love his trunk. It's so soft," she added taking the elephant back in her clasp and stroking it with admiration.

She stared at me as she tenderly stroked her teddy. I was dumbfounded by her boldness. She wanted to be part of the venture I was about to engage in and obviously her only way to do so was to share what she could: her teddy bear collection. Willingly she wanted to give one of her teddies away, admittedly a duplicate, yet by doing so I knew she was with me, all the way.

I squeezed her so tight that evening. Without knowing it, she had propelled me into believing that I could potentially change the world, because if she, an 8-year-old, could understand my quest to help those in need, I had already won half the battle.

Our morning call wasn't the one that I had envisioned. Both tucked in bed, under the warmth of my flowery duvet, I opened my eyes and savoured the details of my sleeping child's face. It wasn't until I looked at my alarm clock that I sat up in distress.

"Shit! Dara, wake up my love. We're late. I didn't hear the alarm. Damn it," I added as I jumped to the floor. I slipped on the clothes I had lazily taken off and left on the floor the night before and headed for the corridor.

"I'm going to make your lunch box, but get your clothes on. Do you have PE today? I think I put a clean pair of shorts in your drawer. And don't forget to brush your teeth!"

Dara seemed completely oblivious. Hiding under the covers, she didn't move. I walked into the kitchen with a thousand thoughts in my mind. Almost like a checklist. Lunch box. School. Cat food. Water plants. Lock the door. Don't forget passport. Call mom. Warm hat. Money.

"Mom! Do you know where my shoes are?" She was up and about.

"Here. Slip these on. I'm ready in five. Are you ready? I didn't put cucumber in your sandwich; I didn't buy anything fresh 'cause I'm leaving. But I have an apple," I mumbled as I slipped my coat on and grabbed my car keys.

We sat silently in the traffic that led us to Dara's school. It was sunny but the cold wind we endured to get to the car had left imprints on our bones. I alternated between sitting on my right and then left hand in an attempt to warm them up. Dara sat still by my side with her hands tucked into the sleeves of her jacket. I turned the radio on, a morning ritual I had adopted ever since I had started to work in the newsroom. It helped me formulate an idea of what I was going to deal with throughout the day. It gave me time to make myself a cup of coffee once in the office, only to be tied to my computer screen for hours on end.

"...The full horror of the human tragedy unfolding on the shores of Europe was brought home this morning..." I looked at Dara to seek for her reaction. I could tell she was aware I was looking at her, but she just looked out straight ahead with a blank look on her face.

"...Images of the lifeless body of a young boy – one of at least 12 Syrians who drowned attempting to reach the Greek island of Kos – reflect the extraordinary risks refugees are taking to reach the West... The picture, taken this morning, depicts the dark-haired toddler, wearing a bright-red T-shirt and shorts, washed up on a beach, lying face down..."[2]

I held my breath. I changed the channel. This wasn't the time to delve into this.

"So, I'll call you when I arrive?" I eventually managed to say as I reached for Dara's right leg. "I'm going via Athens so I'll arrive early evening."

---

[2] The Guardian https://www.theguardian.com/world/2015/sep/02/shocking-image-of-drowned-syrian-boy-shows-tragic-plight-of-refugees

Dara just nodded. Generally, I travelled a lot. I didn't feel absent from her life, it just bothered me that she wanted to travel with me and that I couldn't take her along. Either she was at school, or I was travelling for work. On other occasions I just didn't feel comfortable taking her with me. I had spent the last couple of years exploring the Middle East. I was far from being ready to introduce her to these countries for they were so alive, the cultures so vibrant, the life in these vicinities so simple yet so complicated and perhaps I wanted her to understand the complexities of the region before she set foot in them. But this time was different. I was scared. Any travel is an experience but this time around I was travelling to a humanitarian crisis. No joke.

I shook my head in discontent. My mind drifted to the meeting I had had with Nikki a couple of days back. Nikki was an experienced American relief worker who had just returned from Lesvos herself. Her words rang clearly in my mind.

"What worries me is the threat of cholera developing in one of the camps. People have been using the top of the hill to relieve themselves and now that the rainy season's kicked in, all that waste is making its way down the hill and into the main area of the camp. If any of that waste is contaminated, you're looking at a potential epidemic. It's shocking." She had spoken within the confined walls of a university classroom she had borrowed to inform anyone interested or planning on making their way to Lesvos. She was a big lady, sharp with her words, explicit in her thinking, passionate about humanity yet extremely factual.

Up until that meeting I hadn't thought about the potential health hazard I was walking into. I was more concerned about the health condition of people on the move, their well-being.

"How can we stop this?" I had asked her as I rolled a cigarette. I often sought refuge in my cigarette smoke. In many ways, cigarettes had become my companion. Too many of the cigarettes I smoked went by unnoticed, but some of them, like this one, induced contemplation, assisted me in my processing, gave me a window of time to go within and seek.

"Look, ideally, when you get there, you buy five or six shovels and you find a group of people to dig a trench with you, along the tip of the hill and bury it all. And then you have to try and form some sort of system whereby refugees will bury their waste into the ground each time they relieve themselves. But I've alerted the authorities so I don't think you should worry about that right now."

We were now sitting opposite each other. Everyone else had gone. She was tired from her journey. I could tell she had seen things she wasn't conveying. I sought her reassurance but she wasn't in a position to provide that. She very much stuck with the numbers. She gave away concrete facts. Oliver came to my mind. It struck me how similar they were to each other, particularly at that moment, for I was sure Nikki had an emotional layer to her she wasn't revealing. It was impossible to talk to either of them about what they imagined it felt like to lose your home, your family, your aspirations. Neither of them understood the perpetual void your identity slithers through as you become more and more distant from your childhood memories. I had experienced that feeling on so many occasions and I had found solace in very few people.

"Once you get there, the best thing to do is boil as many eggs as you can, as often as you can. These people are malnourished and weak. Eggs are full of protein and the beauty of them is that they have a shell around them, so you can pass them around, people can keep them for later, they're easy to handle and they can't be contaminated with anything. I've seen volunteers walk on camp giving out chocolates. Sugar's the worse thing to give out to people in distress, particularly when they're coming off the boats, wet, in shock." Shaking her head from side-to-side, she hadn't realised I had drifted away from the conversation.

"It really annoys me when I see thoughtless actions. If you don't know, ask for Christ's sake! So much time and energy is wasted on pointless and at times dangerous initiatives," she paused and watched me light my cigarette as I pulled my eyes away from her. "Just give them eggs, good protein. Nourishment. It's simple," she concluded in a different, calmer tone.

Suddenly I snapped out of my trail of thought and realised we had reached the school gates. I bit my lip in guilt. Once again my mind had travelled to the refugee crisis, disregarding what was going on around me altogether. I should have used this time to connect with Dara. "Damn it Christine," I judged myself.

I jumped out the car and walked around it to reach Dara who was lifting her schoolbag out from the back seat of the car. The badge I had given her stared at me. She had secured it on her bag the day I gave it to her. "Refugees Welcome" it read. I crumbled at the thought of the world I was implicating her in.

"I'll miss you my lovely. You look after yourself and listen to your dad." I squeezed her even harder than I had the night before.

"I will. Bye mom," she smiled, letting go of my embrace. I was hoping she would say something more. What I really wanted was for her to reassure me. To tell me that everything was going to be alright. That she was alright with me leaving. That she understood my calling. That she was aware this was stronger than me. That, somehow, I was also doing this for her. That her generation was the one who would have to deal with the consequences of the crisis. But she was too young. My God, she was too young to understand any of this.

"Love you," I called out as a last resort.

She looked back at me, holding the straps of her rucksack with her two thumbs tucked under her armpits. I could see she was smiling, shyly. "Love you too," she mimed. And on she went through the school gates where one of her girlfriends joined her in her tracks.

I drove home in tears. My imminent departure had begun to loom over me. I had spent so much time looking forward to this moment and now that it had arrived I was revisiting my entire life and everything I was leaving behind as if I were never to return. As if I knew that this journey would ultimately change me; that I would come back with different kinds of baggage and a different person.

For one last time I went through my mental list of things to do before leaving the house. I picked up my cell phone to call my parents. "Mom?" I managed to pronounce as I lifted my rucksack into my car. "Yes, I'm ready, I'm on my way to the airport. I think I have everything." There was a long pause. I wasn't sure why I was calling her unless to say goodbye. I switched the heater on in my car and looked back at my rucksack on the backseat through the rear mirror. I unconsciously did another mental checklist. Passport, yes. Phone, yes. Charger, yes. Money. Got it. I had learnt to deal with my anxiety through reassurance.

"Yes mom, I'm here, sorry, my mind drifted. Yes, yes, I know. What I'm more worried about are these British jet planes flying over us. Do you think this could escalate? They're taking off from Limassol, that's like half an hour away from us... I mean..."

Mom interrupted my thoughts. Somehow she managed to divert the conversation to her cat. I was her only child. It wasn't really fair to worry her like this. "I'll let you know I've arrived safely," I eventually said. "Speak to you soon."

Chapter 3

Finding Lesvos

"Final destination Lesvos? Via Athens?" asked the lady behind the check-in desk at Larnaca International Airport.

I nodded.

"Do you have any hand luggage?"

She peered to the side of the counter.

I nodded.

"Travelling for pleasure?" she smiled courteously. I guess my attire could have implied that. I looked down at what I was wearing: bulky red and black hiking boots, grey combat trousers, my favourite dark blue fleece. I did look like I was going on an expedition. A mountain expedition perhaps.

In contrast to my attire the lady behind the check-in was smartly dressed. Her hair was tightly tied back in a bun, her white and red foulard tickled her chin as she moved her head from side to side. She was pretty and either she loved her job or she made a damn good job at entertaining the idea that she loved her job.

"Yes, pleasure," I smiled at her.

"Oh, I hear it's a beautiful island, apparently it's known for its hot water springs, but there are many refugees in Lesvos. Because of the war, you know? I watch them on TV. So many people are arriving on boats... everyday!" she nodded her head as she dealt with my luggage tag. "It's a big problem..," she continued, "It's sad really, but we can't look after all of them; we can't just let them come into our country and take away our jobs. We're in a financial crisis; we can't even help ourselves, how can we help others?" Her broken English accent irritated me. Or was it just her attitude? I wondered.

"What are *you* doing to help anyway?" I thought to myself as I waited for my boarding pass. "Have you any notion about what these people are going through? Nobody chooses to be a refugee. Do you realise that? Nobody chooses to put their own lives in danger unless it is imperative. *No one puts their children in a boat unless the water is safer than the land*[3]. And people don't just abandon their homes because of war. Do you realise that there are women who flee their homes to escape female genital mutilation? How about the hundreds of people who take a stand against their families to escape forced marriages? Have you heard of human trafficking? Naturally war is a prevalent reason for seeking asylum but there's so much more to this crisis." I paused in my frustration but my thoughts caught up with me. "And you're obviously not Greek. You're Cypriot. How dare you

---

[3] Extract from poem "Home" by Warsan Shire.

speak on behalf of a country you don't even live in! Your country, Cyprus, on the other hand, was divided as a consequence of war, you should be the first one to understand what being a refugee means. How dare you put these people into a single box; you're generalising! You're determining their reality based on yours. You disgust me." I didn't say all of this out loud of course. When she handed me my boarding pass and passport, I smiled, as pleasantly as I could. I paused as I placed my boarding pass between the pages of my passport.

"*No one* would want to be in their shoes," I eventually said, looking at her straight in the eyes. "And if I *were* in their shoes, I surely hope there would be someone out there willing to help me." I fixed the strap on my rucksack which wasn't sitting properly on my left shoulder. "Have a good day *ma'am*," I concluded as I stepped away.

"Next!" I heard her call out as I turned my back.

"Well that went smoothly," I thought to myself. Over the more recent years, I had managed to refrain from engaging in any conversation about refugees. I shot myself in the foot most of the time and anyway, these conversations would almost always end up in a pointless political debate and, as a journalist, I pretended I knew it all. I intimidated people with my know-how. I was so over this.

Mytilini airport looked gloomy. There was a hefty storm brewing outside and by the time I found my way to my rental car in the airport parking I was sopping wet. I sat in the car with the sound of thunder and flashes of lightening as I typed the address of the apartment I had rented into my Google maps app. Initially I had thought of bringing a tent with me and sleeping on camp but Nikki had advised me otherwise. She drilled it into me that it was important I look after myself in order to be able to help those in need. "If you aren't strong, you can't be strong enough for anybody, physically or mentally. Remember that," she had mused.

The narrow road stretched all the way along the coast, a stone's throw away from the seashore. There weren't any streetlights but the moonlight gave away the outline of the sea; white frothy lines dictated the movement of the waters. I wondered if the sea was cold. Within me, I acknowledged that this was the same water the little Syrian boy had battled with before he was found dead on the shores of Kos, not very far away from where I was. I wondered if I should make my way straight to the camp or call it a day and find the apartment.

"I heard that tonight's quiet. The storm. It stops smugglers from crossing the sea," said my landlady as she opened the door for me and handed me the keys to my apartment. She was a middle-aged woman who I was certain looked older than she was. The apartment was on the outskirts of town, a mere ten-minute drive from the main registration camp of the island. The street it was on was a narrow one; the bare stalks of Bougainvillea and dormant jasmine plants adorned the terrace of the building. From where we stood we could hear the echo of the rough sea in the background. I assumed that we were parallel to the sea.

"So, there are another two people sleeping here. They're out now, but they come and go. One man and one woman. You can choose, this bed or that bed. It's up to you. More people are supposed to be coming, tomorrow I believe," said the landlady as we stepped into the apartment. The room was laid out in an 'L' shape with a little kitchenette and a bathroom attached to one side of the room. There were six beds in total; it almost looked like a dormitory. Thick beige woolly blankets everywhere. Apart from the unmade beds and a couple of rucksacks it looked like nobody was actually living here. My landlady was literal when she said people just slept here.

"But what do you mean *it's quiet*? Are there people in the camp?" What I was really asking was whether she thought I should go to the site. I'd reasoned that it was best to drop my bag off and know where I was to sleep before I headed out.

"I don't know. This is what I heard from some of the volunteers this evening, in the city. I've never been to the camp," she explained.

"I'm sorry but what's your name?" I could feel the journalist in me peek its head out.

"I'm Maria," she smiled. It's amazing how far asking someone's name can take you. "I'm Greek, I've lived here all my life, never left Mytilini. But my parents were refugees from Turkey. Before I was born. They came here to build a new life. They built everything from scratch." She divulged all this information as she turned the gas hob on to put the kettle on. It was funny how, although I had rented the apartment, it felt very much like her space, and there was a certain comfort in that. We carried on chatting as I started pulling stuff out from my rucksack: the blue teddy elephant, 20 boxes of anti-inflammatories, 20 boxes of painkillers, 10 packs of period pads, 900 euros I had been donated to make use of in the camp. All stuff Nikki had advised to take with me. Minus the teddy.

"What I think of the most are the women and the children. How they survive this. Yesterday I invited a woman from Afghanistan to come and cook with me in my kitchen. She was so happy. What is life without cooking for your family? Hm? Do you have a family?" she asked me, handing me a freshly brewed fennel tea. It smelt lovely. Homey. I sat down to drink it. I took it as a welcome.

"Yes, I have a family. Nice cup of tea," I cheered to avoid her question. I wasn't here to talk about me. I rarely talked about myself. There was nothing interesting to say about myself anyway. Maria smiled back and then looked at her hands cupping her teacup. I suddenly felt bad because I knew Maria just wanted to chat, company perhaps; I didn't think she was really prying. But I didn't want to get involved. My guard was up. All I wanted was to understand where I was and what was going on.

I've arrived safe my love. Hope you had a good day at school. I miss you already. Love you xxx.

Dara replied to my text message immediately.

D: I'm in bed but I can't sleep. Did you give the elephant away?

C: Why can't you sleep? Tell me, what was the best part of your day? The elephant's sleeping in my bed. I'll find someone tomorrow. Promise xx.

D: I sang in front of my class in show and tell, it was so much fun. Don't forget to tell them the elephant's name (heart).

C: Blueye (heart). I won't. Can't wait to hear you sing to me too. Sleep well my love xxx

Chapter 4

The Truth

I couldn't seem to get my head around what I was supposed to be doing. I was standing in an igloo tent surrounded by dozens of stacked cardboard boxes, suitcases and big black bin bags filled with clothes, shoes, underwear, jackets, jumpers, socks, T-shirts. You name it. But there was no order to anything.

I had made it to the official refugee registration camp known as Moria early that morning. Here, the Greek State, UNHCR, Mercy Worldwide and a number of other NGOs focused on registering and providing aid for Syrian and Arabic speaking refugees. They dealt with the majority of newcomers.

But I soon found out that the official camp had a limited capacity, and considering there were days when we were seeing thousands of people arriving from the shores, their offerings just didn't make do. Early on in the crisis demographics had changed, smuggling routes were now very much in place and there were also hundreds of people coming from other countries than Syria, countries such as Afghanistan, Iraq and Pakistan. The overflow of people arriving at the official camp didn't get any sort of humanitarian aid. They waited for their turn for days on end and whilst doing so they were left without any guidance, without any health care, on their own, in a privately-owned olive grove adjacent to the official camp, on a hill, a place we called the Afghan hill, a place we referred to as the 'outside'.

Assisting people from the 'outside', without the proper infrastructure, guidance, means and ever changing procedures was the challenge that lingered in everyone's mind. Everyone I spoke to that morning shook their heads in awe at what we were witnessing. Most of us were inexperienced and learning as we went along. A young lady who seemed to be somewhat at the helm of activities in the field had explained to me how private money had begun to flow in and that coordination and vision were now crucial in order to move forward. That being 'shut out' from official boundaries was infuriating, for as much as we understood the logic behind maintaining a single authority to lead the way, the truth was that the help provided from the 'inside' wasn't enough. I had seen independent volunteers begging volunteers working for the 'inside' to give them blankets, tents, warm clothes, anything they had. But all the donations the official camp had up its sleeve were locked away in their own warehouses. "We're only permitted to work on state land," I had heard an 'official' volunteer mutter through the barbed wire gates. "We're not allowed to provide any assistance outside these premises."

Regardless, we did what we could with what we could get, and what we were given.

"We need a pair of jeans for a man outside, he's sopping wet. I'd say he's a size 42. He's shaking, I think he's freezing," said Joyce in alarm, who I was manning the makeshift clothes' tent with. She was an elderly lady who had come to help out in the camp seeking for some kind of salvation. I soon realised that every volunteer who came to the camp had some kind of underlying motivation; something to overcome or attain perhaps. She'd been here for a couple of days and taken an avid interest in handing out dry and warm clothes to refugees who came knocking at the tent's door. But there was no system and it was driving me mad. Not only could we not differentiate between varying items of clothing, finding the right sizes was the biggest problem. How was I to find a size 42 pair of trousers in all this mess? Joyce on the other hand had an unbelievably accurate recollection of where she had seen what, but I couldn't work like this. I spent most of the morning folding jackets in one box, jumpers in another, T-shirts in another. I thought about the people who had donated all of these items and what the story behind every item of clothing was. Maybe someone had worn this jumper on their first date, that pair of trousers to their mother's funeral, this T-shirt the day they went into labour. Everything carried some kind of story.

Joyce eventually succeeded in finding the pair of size 42 trousers we were looking for. Once she had given them to the poorly looking man, she left on a break and I focused on sorting out the shoes. Most of the time we were left with stranded pairs of shoes with no match, but when I did reunite a pair, I laid them out in a horizontal line, one pair next to the other, at the entrance of the tent facing outwards, just like one would do in a shop window. There was something so soothing about doing manual work. And it helped because they were more visible like that. Refugees hovered over them, checked the size and walked away with them if they fit their foot. I was chuffed and quite content with myself.

"Marhaba," I heard, hands deep down in a box.

"Marhaba," I answered lifting the tent door, shedding light on who was speaking to me. A tall skinny man, unshaven and handsome, stood in front of me holding his son's hand. Both of them were dressed lightly, nothing appropriate for the temperatures we were facing; the little boy was in sandals.

"This," pointed the father to the row of shoes and his son's bare feet.

"Yes, yes, of course, he must be freezing, let's find you a pair of shoes, hm?" I said to the boy bending down to his height. I was trying to get a better look at the size of his foot for reference. His eyes pierced straight through me. I remembered Dara at his age. He must have been about four years old. I recalled how Dara loved singing and making up words at that age, such joy, energy, silliness, rowdiness. I was puzzled at how this little boy was experiencing all of this.

"What's your name?" I asked him. He was so serious. Shy perhaps or intimidated. His cheeks were red from the cold and his nose was runny and snotty.

He looked at his dad in confusion and reverted to point at his feet.

"Shoes!" I said to him. "Can you say shoes?" I smiled. His dad smiled with me and obviously repeated what I had said in Arabic. But the little boy remained as serious as ever. Right, I thought to myself, I guess that's enough faffing about, let's get this boy some shoes.

"I'll be back, wait for me here," I said turning inwards to the tent.

"Amir!" called out his dad. I looked back. "Ah, Amir!" I exclaimed. "You've got a nice name Amir! Let me find you some shoes!"

I shuffled around in the boxes in despair. Too small, too big, not a pair. Too big, too small, not a pair. Not a pair, too big, too small. And so on. Joyce was still on her break and I was alone manning the tent. I could sense there was quite a bit of people gathering outside the tent. "One-by-one," I said to myself addressing my anxiety, "one-by-one."

"So, Amir, where are you? I think I've found you some shoes," I exclaimed as I got out the tent. I had landed on a brand new pair of Adidas trainers. I was taken aback by the number of people now standing around, all presumably waiting for clothes. I felt pressured to attend to them but I had to deal with Amir first. Amir came running to me and snatched the shoes from my hands.

"Hey!" I said, "You're cheeky," I smiled following his steps. He still wasn't revealing any other emotion, just seriousness. Once he had slipped the shoes on it was obvious they were too small for him. His toes prodded at the top of the shoe and as he took a couple of steps forward, I struggled not to giggle for he looked like a walking duck. Bum in the air, feet wide apart. I watched him go with his dad lingering behind him. I could feel he was smiling too but he nudged my arm and shook his head from side to side. "No good, no good," he muttered.

Of course they were no good, Amir couldn't walk in them. "Amir! We need to change them!" I called out. His dad also attempted to bring him back towards us. And as Amir understood what we wanted him to do, he ignored our calls. A stubborn tantrum that I could easily justify. No one had asked him if he wanted to be here, living in a refugee camp, on a journey to the unknown. But he did choose to want those shoes and I wanted to give his father the prerogative of granting him that. What parent doesn't want to grant their child's wish?

"Wait," I said to his father who was insisting Amir take his shoes off. "Wait here," I said reaching for his arm. He pulled his arm away and looked at me, shocked. I had invaded his private space, intruded on his culture. Crossed a line I knew existed but I was too carried away in the moment to control my self. I attempted to apologise with my eyes; I didn't want them to leave without what they had come for.

"Just wait a minute," I said making the same gesture I would have done had I been trying to tell him to slow down.

Back in the tent I found Joyce frantically in search of something. "Do you know where all the jumpers are? For men? There was a box here, it was filed with warm woolly jumpers."

I was crouched down looking for more shoes, I wanted to find another pair for Amir to take with him. At some point his feet would hurt, for sure.

"Over there," I pointed to Joyce. "Do you think it's okay to give away two pairs of shoes to someone? It's for a little boy," I asked as if I was giving out gold.

"We're here to help Christine, not count our gestures," she replied.

I wasn't counting my gestures, I was just thinking about someone else needing that pair of shoes and not having them anymore.

"Doesn't matter if you touch, one, two, ten or fifty people. What's important is that you touch one. When you've touched the life of one person, you can consider your job done. Whatever you do from there on is more. Excuse me," she nudged. I moved to one side for Joyce to be able to step out of the tent. I couldn't make my mind up. I was torn between sticking to the fact that it was better to give what we had away to those that needed it, even if that meant giving two pairs of shoes to make someone's day, or whether it made more sense to keep things that people had willingly donated just in case someone else needed it. But what if that need never manifested itself? What if we were left with stuff we could have wholeheartedly given away anyway? I realised that as volunteers we preoccupied ourselves with meaningful yet meaningless observations and choices. That this was why procedures and regulations came in handy; because they merely stated your next steps and left no time for thought. Or confusion.

"That little boy is leaving," called Joyce from outside, reminding me of where I was.

Before I stepped out the tent I grabbed Dara's blue elephant from my bag. I handed the extra pair of shoes to the father, he bowed silently and put his hand on his chest. I don't think I'd ever been bowed to before, at least not for doing the necessary. I was usually the one doing the bowing. I bowed as a journalist when I needed to enter public meetings at the very last minute. I bowed as a mother when Dara dispelled her own sense of autonomy. I bowed as a daughter when I understood my parents' true colours. But I had never been bowed to.

Amir on the other hand wasn't bowing although he may as well have been. His reaction to Dara's teddy made me feel humble. For the first time in the past half hour I saw his smile. He held the blue elephant tightly next to his cheek and waved at everyone around us. He waved to me, he waved to his dad, he waved at the lady standing next to me, he waved to Joyce and then he went further along and waved to everyone he encountered. We all giggled as we watched him. My eyes welled up and I fell to my knees as I saw him run back towards me. We remained in an embrace with the blue elephant squeezed in between us for what seemed like a long time. I wished Dara was here. I wished she could have witnessed this. I wished we could have shared this moment with her. I wished she could have met Amir.

Amir waved goodbye with a big smile on his face. "Finally," I thought to myself. He smiled. I turned away from him to make my way back to the tent in contentment. And just as I was somewhat patting myself on the back, a distressed lady called out. She was in the process of standing up from a stone she was sitting on, shoulders back and head looking upwards towards the sky. Her headscarf covered the expanse of her neck but I could tell she was leaning as far back as she could, almost begging for something to reach her from the skies. I slowly made my way to her without her noticing. She was concentrated on what she was doing, almost as if in a trance. Once a couple of steps away from her, she felt my presence. She brought her head down slowly and eventually turned towards me.

"Hi," I said softly. And before I managed to say anything more, she lifted both her arms up at a ninety degree angle, stretched them out in front of her, put the palms of her hands together and clasped her fingers into a fist. As she pressed her two index fingers together, she eventually pointed her arms towards me and in slow motion began to imitate the sound of a firing gun.

"Rat, ta, ta, ta, ta, ta, ta!" she repeated and her arms shook up and down. I froze in my being.

"Rat, ta, ta, ta, ta, ta, ta!" she repeated.

And again: "Rat, ta, ta, ta, ta, ta, ta!"

I was incapable of saying a single word. The thought of interrupting her jolted me. I just let her be until she brought her hands back down to the sides of her body. We paused for a while, we looked at each other until I decided to approach her and take her in an embrace. She naturally allowed me to invade her space. I held her tight as she cried like a baby in my arms. I felt her tears rolling down her face and falling lightly into my neckline, and as my hair stood on end at the thought of what made her hurt so deeply and so much, she spoke softly in a language I couldn't understand, without stopping. I held her there for what seemed a long time, I had closed my eyes and just listened to the music of her words until Joyce joined us ever so quietly. She asked me what was going on as she put her left hand on the woman's back and pulled my hair away from her face.

"We need a translator," I told Joyce in a low voice. "Dari. I think she's from Afghanistan," I added.

Joyce nodded and walked away, understanding what I was asking for. I watched her make her way down the hill towards the centre of the camp. It was cold and people had started lighting fires in barrels volunteers had collected from town. Residents of the camp had gathered around the barrels, squatted and rubbed their hands together as they briefly spoke to each other and smoked countless cigarettes. It looked as if they spent more time staring at the ground than anything else. Contemplating their next steps I assumed.

The lady was still talking down my neck. We remained

in the same embrace until Joyce and a translator came back. We spent a long time listening to her story, her distress. The translator let us know that her name was Wida; that she was travelling alone. It was very unusual for women to be travelling on their own through migration routes such as this one. It was men who led the way, it was men who dealt with smugglers and money. It was men who approached strangers and Wida was stuck in this reality. She hadn't spoken to anyone in the past six weeks except for the bus drivers and the smugglers. As she explained, she begged for food in silence. She had been doing everything in silence since she had seen her entire family shot in front of her eyes, hence her initial recounting of a gun firing when I first approached her.

Her husband, mother and two children had been shot outside of their home while Wida was inside the house. For some reason they never went after her. Her husband had been outspoken and criticised the government. He was against the oppression in Afghanistan. It cost him his and his family's life and Wida ran for her own. It took her almost two months to make her way to Turkey. She travelled mostly by foot, but found her way on a bus a couple of times until she reached the coast in between Turkey and Greece. 2000 euros she paid to a smuggler to bring her to the Greek shores. And here she was. Standing at the top of a hill, in an olive grove, in the cold, alone, frightened, unsure of her next steps, in my embrace. What was I to do?

As the translator continued to listen to Wida, Joyce

and I decided to go and speak to someone within the state registration camp. Inside the camp there were NGOs who dealt exclusively with women and offered them support. It was obvious that Wida wasn't in a sound mental state and we felt it was important for her to have a break before continuing on her journey and hopefully connect with other women. It took a lot of convincing for Wida to agree to come with us to seek help. I was surprised by the fact that she had no belongings with her. Just a plastic bag.

"I have no one to call," she told us as she pulled her phone out of her pocket. "It's no use to me anymore."

With a heavy heart, I left Wida with a social worker. The sound of the gun she had made stuck in my mind and I felt the depth of her solitude in my core. I slept very little that night. Squinting my eyes shut I recalled the sight of Dara's blue elephant which had lain on my pillow until that very morning. I thought of Amir. I whispered words to Wida in my mind. I silently said I was sorry to her so many times. I hoped she was warm and fed and surrounded by good people. I hoped that revealing her story would alleviate her pain, even if just a little. I thought about what tomorrow would bring. Who would cross my path and how I would manage to help those who did, if I could. I was anxious about tomorrow yet alert at its potential offerings and I felt strong even though I was physically tired. Exhausted should I say.

Chapter 5

The Storm

There were days in the camp that were easier than others. There were also nights that were quieter than others. The weather played an important role in this. It was pertinent that the sun enlightened our spirits. When the sun was out we moved around in the camp and talked to each other more. The relief that came with hanging things out to dry, whether that be blankets or sleeping bags, trousers and socks, jumpers or mattresses, or the actual ground we were standing on, was contagious. But sunny days also meant more arrivals. Smugglers took advantage of the sunny weather to cross the sea and that was the catch-twenty-two.

Every morning, as I boiled dozens of eggs in my apartment, I listened to the news on the radio until the end so that I could listen to the weather forecast. That's a lie. I listened to the news to make sure that the world I had come from was still alive. As days passed, less and less made sense simply because it was impossible to compare anything to anything.

"An approximate two thousand refugees arrived in Lesvos yesterday, reaching almost 450,000 refugees who have passed through the island this year, an unprecedented number..." I switched the radio off.

These bloody numbers. What do numbers reveal to anyone except alarm anyway? I resented the way media made use of numbers to blow things out of perspective. They manipulated them, they abused them. I had spent the whole day in the camp and I was tired but I never felt quite right spending time in the apartment. Cooking food, taking a shower, sleeping in a bed, using a toilet. It all felt too luxurious, my surroundings felt somewhat awkward. There were people literally sleeping out in the open, with no shelter, in the freezing cold. We had managed to find big empty metal barrels and bought trucks full of wood to make fires in them and give warmth, provided it didn't rain. It felt ludicrous sitting here in my sanitised, warm and homey apartment.

My phone rang. It was Arthur. Arthur was half English, half Mexican, an avid professional photographer and musician who had come to Lesvos out of pure impulse. A little like me minus all the frustration. In the camp, he really didn't do much other than chat to refugees and take photographs. He'd actually captured some beautiful portraits. Which was great; there's nothing more human than talking and connecting with people. He sure was curious. But as I'd told Oliver on the phone when he had asked me to report back for the newspaper, I personally couldn't sit around and talk to refugees in the camp, never mind interview them. We were in the midst of a humanitarian crisis, and I felt that my duty went beyond depicting their pain. In many cases we were attending to matters of survival. But that was Arthur; a people's person. He was comfortable with focusing on the benefits of reporting stories and visuals to wider audiences. He believed that by doing so, funding would be more accessible, that by placing the crisis in the limelight, more volunteers and organisations that supported displaced people would be heard and supported. And he was right; he simply had different boundaries from me. He cared immensely but he had a way of not getting personally involved in things, he knew when to step back whereas I would walk straight into things without looking left or right. Every person has a role, even in a crisis, and he made sure I remembered that when I lost track of what we were doing. It's also from Lesvos that he had managed to have his photographs published in The Guardian. There was no denying that he, too, reaped benefits. But he remained modest about it.

"Hello?" I answered getting to my feet. Every phone call I received on my Greek number was an emergency, hence the jitteriness.

"Hey! How's it going?" revealed that there was no pressing urgency. Arthur was always chirpy. Bold smile. Big beautiful eyes. He was often the heart of the room when there were more than the two of us in the apartment. Arthur had been around since I had arrived on the island so I felt most comfortable with him. Everyone else in the flat seemed to come and go. It seemed as if nothing fazed him. Always positive. Never in doubt. Always on the go.

"D'you wanna come with me to Molyvos tomorrow morning? Early? I haven't done the boats yet and I really want to see it in action. Take some photos of the refugees as they come off the boats onto the shore. And there's also that life-jacket graveyard, I'd like to go and see that too. Shall I wake you? We need to set off early though, like 5am or something; it'd be cool if we got there by sunrise." We had talked about going to Molyvos on so many occasions, but I felt such a duty to the different tasks I was undertaking in the camp that I never actually followed through.

"You don't 'do the boats' Arthur... Jesus... how can you just say it like that?" I was nitpicking by this point, so many volunteers just came for the ride. It reminded me of a bunch of Scottish students who had come to the camp very early one morning asking how they could help. We suggested that they head to town and make as many sandwiches as they could with the budget that they had. They had come back with the boot of their car filled with cheese and ham sandwiches. Little did they know that most Muslims don't eat ham and 90 percent of people on camp were Muslim. "What a waste," I recalled.

"You there?" questioned Arthur.

"Yeah, sorry, I'm here, I'm just a bit tired," I lied.

"Did you hear anything I said?" I spent most of my time lost in thoughts these days. This wasn't the first time Arthur had asked me that very same question. "Did you hear anything I said?" he repeated. I bit my lip.

"No. I mean, yes. Of course. Of course I'll come with you in the morning. I'll put my alarm clock on. But

47

I'm not shadowing you with that camera. I'll do my own thing."

"Yes! Sure, cool. You do your thing. I'll see you in the morning. Good night Chris."

I hung up the phone with a knot in my stomach. I wasn't ready to face the shores. In the newsroom, I had edited too many photos of people painstakingly disembarking from makeshift dinghies. Blue and orange auras fluttered in my vision. I sat down. I stood up again. I drank a big glass of water as I held on to the kitchen top. As I put the glass back down on the counter my car keys were right next to my hand. I stared at them. I grabbed them. I walked out of the door.

Driving up to the camp I drove past a family of five. Man, woman and three children. Although it was pitch dark I caught a glimpse of the mother sitting on the ground and the father kneeling in front of her, holding his arms out in front of him and over her shoulders, taking care of her. The camp was a steady climb up on a hill. Throughout the day I had seen dozens of people making their way up on foot. "Could they be trying to make their way up there? They're struggling," I thought to myself with underlying concern. Something wasn't right. There was a bus service that usually transported people from the shore to the camp. I wasn't sure why so many people opted not to use the bus. Unless the buses were full. The past couple of days had seen a surge in arrivals. I stopped dead in my tracks. As I did a U-turn, a police car drove past me. I took no notice of it as I pressed on my emergency light button and made my way back towards the family.

"Are you okay?" I said bending down next to the mother. She was veiled and her head was hidden in her hands. I looked up at the children's bare faces, then turned to the father.

"Moria," he said.

"Yes, yes, Moria. The camp. You want to go to the camp?" I took the mother in my embrace, helping her to her feet. She was holding her right leg and was obviously in quite a lot of pain. "I'll take you to Moria," I asserted pointing to the car. "I'll take you. With the car. To Moria." I felt I had to repeat everything I said twice or three times. I spoke ever so slowly. I had no idea what they were thinking or if they understood what I was saying but the father urged his children to follow him to the car; the youngest one must have been no more than four years old.

As soon as they were settled in the car, the cops parked a couple of metres further down, head on.

"Your driving licence please," demanded one of the policemen. They had obviously had the same sixth sense as I did.

"What are you doing in Lesvos?" he insisted as he scanned my papers. I knew that approach all too well. There was nothing wrong with my driving licence, the car was rented under my name. I wasn't speeding. What was he getting at? I decided to take a friendly approach.

"Oh," I smiled, "I'm here on holiday. Visiting." The police officer ducked down and peered through my car window.

"Are they travelling with you?"

So *they* were the problem, not me, I realised.

"You probably noticed them on your way up, they're trying to get to Moria," I nonchalantly revealed. "Thought I'd give them a lift. These young children have no business walking up this dark road in the middle of the night. I'm just going to drop them off." I smiled in full confidence and that was as much as I wanted to share with him. Neither did I want to tell him that I was a journalist, nor that I was working in the camp. I was surprised by my need to remain incognito. It was almost as if I felt guilty of my presence.

"I'm afraid I'm going to have to ask you to ask all passengers not travelling with you to get out of the car, Miss Tillard. Or we can meet at the police station," said the policeman as he handed me back my driving licence.

"Excuse me?" I objected.

"It's illegal to have unregistered migrants in your car Miss Tillard. And from what I understand they are unregistered seeing as they're making their way to camp. Unless you want to ask them if they have official papers for each of them?" The smirk on his face told me I had no power but I couldn't resist.

"I'm unaware of such regulations," I slowly muttered

trying to phrase my next sentence. "The lady next to me has a knee injury and I'd say the children are quite young. Do you really think it's wise to let them find their own way? It's a five minute drive." Intentionally I had switched to Greek in an attempt to bring his guard down.

"You've got a good Cypriot accent for a Belgian," he chuckled.

"Ugh, he already knows more about me than I can handle," I thought to myself. The kids were mumbling to their father in the back seat. "Shhh, shhhh," was all I could make out while the mother remained ever so still with her fingers clasped in between one another. I was stuck in between telling the policeman to mind his own business and asking the family to get out the car. Neither felt right. I visualised driving off without driving over the policeman's feet.

I sat back in the driver's seat and leant my head back, closing my eyes for a minute. With my right index finger I lifted the car window button and listened to the sound of the window making its way up and closing shut. That was the only gesture I could muster to convey my thoughts to the policeman; put a wall between us. We weren't the same species, he and I. We stood in parallel worlds. He was doing his cold-hearted job, I was clutching at straws. He watched me as the car window physically divided us. With all my courage I turned to my side from where I could see everyone in the car.

"I'm really sorry but I can't take you to Moria." What

a joke. Surely I had never intended to give them false hope. "You have to get out the car." I ploughed through my directions without a word of a lie. But nobody moved. The mother started crying at my side. The policeman stood motionless outside my window. I stepped out of the car in full force. He took a step back and watched my next moves. I walked to the passenger door. Once the door open, I bent down and took the mother's hand in mine.

"I'm sorry, you must get out the car; for now. But I'll go to camp and see what I can do." I was lying. I couldn't think of anything I could legitimately do. I was surprised by my need to lie. Why did I feel the need to lie about my not being able to help? It wasn't the first time I had felt the urge to, as if lying would make things easier. In truth, lies in these situations brought more disappointment to them once they realised you weren't coming back for them, that you couldn't help them on their journey even though you said you would, that even though you had made out you could turn the tables around you actually couldn't. And I was no hero in all of this yet this need to lie almost tried to affirm that I was, thus implying that I wasn't actually lying for them but I was lying for myself, to make *me* feel better, to justify *my* actions, to define *myself*. The policeman peered over the car as if acknowledging what I had just said. I nodded at the father, instigating their move.

Driving off I watched the family's distinct silhouette through my rear view mirror. I held the steering wheel with my knees and rolled myself a cigarette. I was seething with anger, hurting with despair, I re-enacted the whole scenario searching for a loophole. The police car drove steadily behind me up until I parked outside the camp. I took long drags of my cigarette as I waited for them to disappear. What I was really thinking was whether I should risk going back to get the family.

"Christine!" someone was banging on my car window in thick black gloves. "Christine!" I lowered my window with a cloud of smoke coming out in a vacuum.

"Christine! I'm so glad you're here. We need your help. There are hundreds of people making their way from the shore. The buses are full and some of them are making their way here on foot. The soup is ready but there are so many people, we need more people to man the tent. You up for it?" Ralph looked stressed. Overworked. He'd funded and set up a grassroots 24-hour soup tent in the camp to provide warmth and partial hunger relief. It seemed to take everything out of him. Fixing his red bandana he leant back on the side of the car and gazed across the street.

"Look!" he paused in awe.

"Jesus." I stepped out of the car and threw my ciga-rette to the ground as I locked the car. The access to the camp was a steep tarmac road. From where we stood there were hundreds of people making their way to the tip of the hill. Gold and silver hyperther-mia blankets dotted the crowd; the crippling sound they were making pierced right through me. Should I have closed my eyes, I could have sworn I was outside a stadium, making my way to the ticket box of a pop concert. But these people weren't making their way to any ticket box; they weren't buying just any ticket, they were buying tickets to their fate.

"Come on, let's go!" I locked my arms with Ralph's and began to make a move towards the tent. It was freezing cold, dark and humid.

"The problem is," explained Ralph who was running short of breath, "the two big cauldrons of soup just outside the tent are too close to the residents of the camp who are coming to get served. The mass is pushing forward and I'm worried they're going to push the boiling hot cauldrons over or, that one of us is going to catch alight from one of the big gas hobs. We need to find a way to push them back, but you'll see... there's so many people..." He paused as we pushed on through the crowd. Our arms unlocked with each other, they reunited again. We moved gracefully but fast. Our conversation seized and then started again on a couple of occasions. "I've got an idea and you're the only one who can help me right now."

I felt the stress driving me forwards; that feeling of eagerness to deal with a situation but I was doubtful as to how we were going to go about this.

"Maybe we could stretch a rope across the front of the cauldrons or something, like a dividing line that would separate them from the tent," I proposed off the top of my head. We were now standing at the tip of the hill looking down to where we could see the camp tucked away in the hill towards our right. We actually couldn't see the tent; it was hidden by an extended semi-circle of people that had been formed around its entrance. A single faint light was shining from within the tent, the only indication of its presence.

"There's no time for that Christine," snapped Ralph. "Look, you're a woman. You can manage this." He said, grabbing me by the shoulders in a standstill. I looked at him in query. What did any of this have to do with the fact that I was a woman? I tried to step back but he was holding me so tight I couldn't move.

"I need you to go and stand right at the entrance, just as you would if you were standing at the tip of a boat. I want you to stand tall and confident. And when you're ready I want you to call out, as loud as possible. Speak to the people. Are you listening?" he asked me as I looked back and forth from his eyes to the tent.

"I don't understand what this has to do with the fact that I'm a woman. *You* speak to them!" I released his hands from my shoulders.

"Christine, wait, wait! Hear me out, I'm really serious. Listen. Listen!" He had raised his voice. In many ways I wanted to throw it all back in his face and tell him this was no way to talk to a woman. I would have said anything to get out of the situation and blocking him with my womanhood felt like a good opportunity to deflect his wants. But he had caught my attention in his despair.

"You're a woman and they'll respect you a thousand times more than they would any man. I want you to stand there and *tell* them that you're a woman and demand that they form a line. Help them get in some kind of order. Trust me Christine, I *know* this can work. A man will less likely lash out at a woman trying to feed him. And I'll be right behind you." He sought for my gaze in an attempt to figure out what I was thinking, how I would respond.

"Is this some kind of a joke? You want me to stand there and use my womanhood as bait? Whatever happened to gender equality and all that shit? Are you fucking kidding me?" I shuffled on the spot gaining grounds for what I thought was a feminist debate unrolling.

"Christine. Christine. Calm down. We're not here to negotiate your womanhood. Listen!" he was getting impatient and I was obviously ignoring the urgency of the situation. I lifted my head up, took a deep breath and scanned the people around me. All I could see was faces of disbelief.

"Jesus, Ralph," I eventually said.

"Come on, grab my hand. You'll be fine." We ran down the hill. In less than a couple of minutes I found myself in front of dozens of hungry, cold and desperate beings. With a cauldron on each side of me I could now see the danger Ralph was foreseeing. The force of the crowd was powerful and forthcoming. Two volunteers, Peter and Ahmed, were handing out paper cups of soup, one by one, with hands coming at them from all sides.

"Stand back!" called Ahmed as he poured the soup in paper cups, "stand back!" His words fell on deaf ears. Ralph came up behind me, and in a very gentle voice, with his reassuring hands on my shoulder, pushed me forward and said, "You've got this Christine. You can do it."

It took me a couple of seconds before I realised I was holding my breath. "Breathe Christine, breathe," I thought to myself. Standing at the edge of my comfort zone I silently said, "I'm a woman, please stand in a line."

"Louder," encouraged Ralph from behind me.

"I'm a woman, please stand in a line," I repeated with a little more vocal power.

"That's my girl, now say it again, a little louder," Ralph insisted.

As if my heart had broken I took another deep breath, I thought of nothing as I now shouted, to the very best of my capabilities, "I AM A WOMAN, PLEASE STAND IN A LINE!" My call was met by a young Afghan's eyes. He looked straight at me and dropped his arms to the sides of his body as if telling me he was ready to take a lead. He turned to his right and said something in Dari to a man standing beside him. In turn, he moved behind him as he grabbed another man and pushed him behind him too.

"Now follow that line," Ralph nudged me forward, "and keep on repeating the same thing. It's working, they'll follow your lead. Go, Christine. Go!"

I stepped forward bowing at the young Afghan. "I'm a woman," I paused. "Please stand in line," I continued. And as I stepped on forward, a line of men was forming to the right of my shoulder. I continued walking up the hill as it all miraculously happened in front of my eyes. I couldn't believe my steps, and I couldn't look back, I just carried on moving forward, calling out what had become some sort of mantra, a meditation that called me forward until I reached the tip of the hill. Once at the tip, I hesitantly turned around and saw the line of humans standing in front of my eyes. My eyes welled up. What had I done? I was astounded at what I had accomplished, how my presence had managed to goad people into action, and the result almost horrified me. Human lines recalled education, oppression, power. I wasn't one to impose my being. Or impose my wants; oblige people to do things. The only thought that soothed my conscience was the sensation of soup making its way down my throat, into my belly, into my well-being, a warmth I prayed would reach each and every person that stood before me. For they deserved it.

Chapter 6

Selfies & Ambiguities

I woke up to the smell of coffee. Arthur was packing his camera bag. Everyone else in the apartment was fast asleep. I had dreamt that I was carrying terracotta pots filled with big bright red strawberries. Throughout the entire dream I walked through quaint narrow pedestrian streets freely handing out the strawberries to people I encountered on my way, random strangers, one-by-one. I was enveloped by the miracle of nature, how its fruits could offer delight to people's taste buds and hunger. The dream transcended such a lightness to my being, yet the thought that there wasn't enough for everybody propelled a feeling of guilt in me; there was never to be enough strawberries for everybody, and I woke up with the fear that nature itself was running out. Shying away from the rays of daylight coming through the curtains of the window opposite me, I clasped at my dark blue duvet, cherishing the last couple of minutes I had before I would have to walk out of the door only to venture into another type of dream; the likes of the Mediterranean shores and seas that silently held the crossings of so many brave souls.

"What do you think the Mediterranean Sea would

say if we asked her how she feels about carrying all these people on the move?" I sluggishly whispered to Arthur as he made sure I was awake. I knew he was anxious to get going but I wasn't quite ready to face the day or the shores.

"Refugees you mean?" he asked me, placing a cup of hot sweet coffee by my bed.

Refugees, migrants, asylum seekers, economic migrants. Opportunists someone had once told me. Ugh, I couldn't differentiate between any of these categories anymore.

"You know what I mean," I said sitting up in bed attending to my coffee cup.

"You take things too personally, Christine," said Arthur sitting on the edge of my bed. "Sure, the sea holds many secrets. In many ways, or philosophically, it probably understands much more than we do. As you said, one day she'll have much more to reveal about climate refugees. This is only the beginning. I can't fathom what's going to happen when more people start moving because they have no more water. No more land. Too much heat," he paused as he examined his shoes, moving his feet from side to side. "Damn girl, it's a bit early to get into this, hm? Drink up, we need to make a move." He stood up and left me lingering in my thoughts.

By 6am we were driving along the coast looking out to sea. The weather was crisp but clear. Arthur had already talked on the phone to a couple of people who spent their days on the lookout for boats that were approaching the island. I often wondered what difference it made to know how many boats were making their way to us; they were coming whatever the case. That morning there were three boats making their way to the shores. I was shocked at how close Turkey was from us. On clear days like that morning, we could see the landforms of the Turkish coastline with our bare eyes. And yet a number of migrants never made it across.

"So what's the deal with you anyway?" pondered Arthur holding the steering wheel with his right hand and a shitty pre-packed cold coffee in the other.

"What?" I asked, wondering what he was getting at.

"Well, what's a top notch journalist, single mom, fiercely stubborn and independent woman like you looking for? Here? And don't give me all that talk about side-tracking from journalism or wanting to change the world. What is it that you're really looking for?" It was astounding how raw the friendships I made at the camp were. As if despair stripped us to our core, filtered away any form of barriers; we spoke our truth with no inhibitions. There was nowhere to hide from the fact that all of us working in the camp were fortunate, that the path we had been handed in life was a smooth one, however much we dismissed it. Our materialistic pursuits justified none of our whims. The rawness of what we were witnessing grounded us in a flash, left us with no other bearings than our humility and humanity.

It took a long time for me to formulate my thoughts. It took me an even longer time to answer. It never occurred to me that there was something deeper to my decision to make my way to Lesvos. And Arthur was hitting the nail right on the head.

"Home," I whispered, unsure of what I was divulging.

"Home?" shrugged Arthur.

"When you've been uprooted from your home, by no choice of your own, there's a forever void within your heart, like a longing for something you know nothing about really -a lie you formulate in your mind in order to make sense of the 'new' place you've come to call home. As time, or years go by, that lie holds on to nothing but a memory. And there where you felt you 'belonged' to somewhere, you realise you don't, because your references become bleak, you mature with time and whatever you pick up along the way eventually doesn't correspond to what you left behind anymore. And so home becomes a philosophy, an ephemeral notion that's tied to so many things: family, childhood, friendships, smells, atmospheres, traditions, even street names for God's sake... A lifestyle that sits solely within your heart and which you carry with you everywhere you go but can't precisely comprehend."

Arthur listened attentively. I could tell he was intrigued but he said nothing to interrupt me. I was delving into the depths of my soul, trying to figure out why people on the move touched me so much.

I was also coming to terms with why Arthur consistently told me that I took things too personally.

"Not every one here lost their home through no choice of their own Christine." It was a poignant response.

"Of course not. Let's not become customs officers who differentiate between Syrians and Palestinians, Afghans and Africans, Pakistanis and Iraqis, Arthur. You're missing the point," I objected.

"Fine, but you too recognise that countries can't absorb the massive influx of people we're witnessing. Look at Germany, look at Greece, look at Lesvos, here, now, where we are as we speak. It's unfair for the local population to have to cope with this. There are more migrants here than local inhabitants!"

"Yes! I know, I'm a taxpayer too, Arthur. Don't think that I would willingly give away what I have worked for all my life, not that I have much," I paused making a mental note that it was usually those who had money who hungered for more. "... Nor would I compromise my daughter's safety, the freedom that she holds at her front door. I'm not negotiating that."

"But you are!" interrupted Arthur.

"No! I'm not. I'm not talking on behalf of any government, or system or power, Arthur. Not even as a journalist. I'm talking from a purely human perspective. Don't you get it? Doesn't anyone get it? I'm tired of having to fight over this. Fuck. At the end of the day, we're talking about human rights here. People have a right to movement, and that's a fact. Jesus, Arthur, your grandparents were Mexicans and now you call yourself a Brit! Give me some credit here. Is Mexico home for you or is England home for you? Or should I say London? That's even worse! You were born and brought up in diversity. Don't give me this shit!"

There was tension in the car. It always boiled down to the same damn thing. But I felt powerless in this discussion. I wasn't here to change the system. I can't count the number of protests I've been to in demand of whatever: employment rights for asylum seekers, stop the war in Syria. I had been protesting with individuals outside the Ministry of Interior for family reunification. I just didn't see things as black and white. It was about not allowing anyone to suffer, it was about preserving dignity and yes, the right to dream of a better life, even if that life is sought elsewhere from where you were born.

As I looked out the car window I began to silently recite Maxime Le Forestier's lyrics. *We don't choose our parents, we don't choose our family, We don't choose the sidewalks of Manila, Paris or Algeria to learn how to walk. To be born somewhere... to be born somewhere for the one who is born is always a coincidence...*

"Boats! Christine, to your right! Can you see them? There! In the distance!" Arthur steered to the side of the road and stopped the car. We both got out and ventured to the edge of the cliff, looking out to sea. Three black inflatable dinghies dotted with people wearing bright orange life vests. The sea was choppy

from the wind, the boats swayed in a peculiar fash-
ion. They weren't swaying from side to side, nor back
and forth. They floated in a kind of dance that resembled the twist but in slow motion. There was no
way to count how many people there were on the
dinghies but the people sitting on the periphery of
the boats looked as if they were almost hanging off
the sides. To our left, the coast stretched way down
below us and at the far edge of the peninsula there
was a mass of people scattered on the shore, a couple
of cars, a makeshift white tent, nothing much really
besides the glory of the depths of the turquoise blue
Mediterranean Sea.

"Let's go down there," offered Arthur, "there must
be access as we drive closer." The cliff was jagged and
rough, an approximate 15-metre drop. The shore was
made up of grey and black pebbles; it looked wild
and unapproachable. By the time we made our way
down to the shore, on foot it turned out, the dinghies
weren't far from the shore, slowly drifting towards us
with the current. We all stood waiting. I noticed almost all of us were standing up straight, with our feet
apart, hands down the sides of our body, except for
a lady who was biting her nails. A little beyond us,
two men stood at the edge of the sea holding walkie
-talkies in their hands and wearing knee high plastic
fishing boots. They were estimating about 80 people
per dinghy. We were expecting about 120 people
amongst whom were children and elderly people. I
had no idea how to proceed. I stood back. I looked
around me seeking for something to do but there was
nothing to do until they actually arrived on land. I

approached a lady who was standing beside me. She looked calm but sceptical. I was sure she had done this before. Coming closer to her, I turned towards the sea and stood at her side, almost imitating her.

"We need to get the children and elderly people off first, get them hyperthermia blankets... there's a volunteer doctor in the tent if needed," the lady pointed to the tent and began to walk forward. "We should get as close as possible to the shore," she added in a matter-of-fact way. We both wore heavy winter jackets, our combat trousers battled in the wind. Our noses were red from the cold yet the sun was shining. As we stood there, we could hear the people on the dinghy calling out, many of them frantically waved at us as though we hadn't seen them. Some tried to stand up and then fell back down again, rocking the dinghy as they righted themselves. It was eerie to watch them approach. I worried about their safety but I was more anxious about what would happen to them from here on. Where would they go once they had reached the shore?

When the two men had managed to get their hands on the first dinghy, they called out to us. Four people had already jumped overboard, ploughing their way through the water towards the land. At the bow of the boat was a woman holding a well wrapped baby; a tiny little white bundle no wider than her thorax. I looked at her anguished face, her jeans were wet up to her knees and her headscarf flowed in the wind, hiding her face and shoulders from time to time.

"The mother and infant! Help them to shore," said

one of the men. He was looking in my direction. I had to look behind me before I realised he was actually talking to me. More and more people jumped off the boat as they understood that the water was shallow enough for them to walk through. Commotion reigned; voices came at us from all sides, the dinghy rocked up and down, hands reached out at us, the sea water was seeping through my clothes, everyone was cold but there was no time to think about that. I turned back towards the shore as I held on to the hand of someone trying to get off the boat. As I turned around to lead them to the shore, I caught a glimpse of two people lying on a blanket on the pebbly beach. I couldn't figure out if they had fainted or what the problem was. There were a couple of people hovering over them, wrapping them in hyperthermia blankets. The doctor was nowhere to be seen. A little further down, a lady was handing out hot cups of tea from a big thermos as she invited them to sit on the rocks and press pause on their lives. In so many ways I wanted time to stand still for a minute, just to get my bearings. Everything was happening so fast.

"Come closer, come closer!" insisted the man from afar who was now holding the mother's hand. She was still standing tall in the dinghy. She wasn't confident. "Grab the baby, I'll help her down," he continued as I trod in the ice-cold sea and felt my boots and socks submerge in water once again. I lifted my arms towards the mother. She was hesitant for a minute. "It's okay, it's okay, she will bring your baby to shore, give her your baby," instructed the man making gestures with his arms. She turned to her husband and

questioned him in Arabic. They spoke to each other for some time while her husband stared at me,
straight into my eyes. I could tell they were negotiating whether it was okay to hand their child over to an
absolute stranger. Still holding my arms out, my jaw
chattering, I nodded as I repeatedly told them it was
okay, I spoke with a loud voice but there was so much
going on I couldn't hear myself speak. The man was
getting irritated, the people on the other two boats
were also beginning to disembark. There was a sea of
people desperate to move forward; some helped each
other, others pushed on forward shoving people out
of their way.

"Come on!!" shouted the man. He had lost his patience. "You need to get out now, you're here! Other
people are waiting behind you," he insisted in a more
self-contained manner. That's when I noticed an elderly woman on board leaning on a young boy. She
was shivering all-over. Wrapped in a sheet, she looked
down at the centre of the boat with an expressionless
look on her face. "The elderly woman!" I called to
the man, "the elderly woman!" I repeated, speaking
over my right shoulder, still holding my arms up. I
looked at him in panic, I was afraid for the elderly
woman. The young boy she was leaning on just sat
there holding her hands. He was in shock, I assumed.
Motionless. In disbelief.

"Grab it!" I'd lost track of what I was doing and the
man was calling me to my senses. The mother had finally decided to hand me her child. As I clasped my
arms around the tiny infant, I felt the white blanket

was sopping wet and ice cold. A shiver ran down my spine. The baby's face wasn't visible, it was so well wrapped in the sheet from head to toe. "Jesus," I thought to myself. I walked out of the sea holding the bundle tight in my arms. "She's wet," I called out, "we need dry clothes," I continued. For some reason I had decided the infant I was carrying was a little girl, the edge of the blanket was pink. I looked around trying to meet someone's eyes to direct me. Tell me where I could find dry clothes, relieve me from the burden of carrying a stranger's baby. I had never ever touched a stranger's baby without consent and I was petrified as to what I would find if I unwrapped the bundle. "What if she's dead," I thought to myself in alarm. I decided I would make my way to the tent. Find the doctor. As I walked against the wind I turned back to see if her mother and father were following me. Absorbed in my duty, I had forgotten about my bundle's parents. As I turned around, I stood still holding the baby ever so tightly. I scanned what lay before me; dozens of people where frantically finding their way. I looked for the mother's beige headscarf which had marked her identity in my mind, but she wasn't the only one wearing a headscarf. There were so many women wearing headscarves. "Shit, where the fuck is she?" I panicked. I began to retrace my footsteps until the couple caught my attention. They were standing apart from the crowd, in an embrace. The woman was holding her cell phone up, smiling at it while she lay her head on her husband's shoulder. She kissed him on the cheek and took another photo as she indulged. "For fuck's sake, it's them." I muttered. I couldn't believe what they were doing. "Your baby!" I called out to them. "She's wet! You have to get her warm... hello?" I continued making my way to them but they paid no attention to me. They continued to take selfies.

I stopped in my tracks. I looked down at the bundle in my arms that had begun to cry. It was the first time in my life I was so happy and moved to hear someone cry, for her voice confirmed that she was alive and that was all that mattered. "Yes baby, yes, it's going to be alright," I whispered, bringing the bundle higher up towards my cheeks. Slowly I unwrapped the white blanket to reveal her face, and there she was, as white and fragile as porcelain, looking up at me with her dark poignant eyes. Her glance told me everything and nothing at the same time. The sound of the sea caught my attention. For the first time since the morning, I felt I was alive, hopeful. The eyes of a child, her unconditional being amongst the raw reality we found ourselves in, told me that looking at the crisis on a one-on-one basis was the only way forward, that I would fight in solidarity for anyone seeking a better life, righteously or not, legally or not, modestly or not, I didn't give a shit. If Europe wanted to close its borders so be it. "You close your borders Europe, you're a fine example of democracy aren't you? You spread fear of the other wherever you spit but I'll stand guard against your violence. I'll spit back at you with as much love as my chest can boast. And I'll defy you. I'll defy your vision for you have none other than greed. I'll defy you with my mortality. No child deserves to die on these shores. No innocence should be shattered in between and amongst borders." I ploughed through my anguish.

"My baby!" I suddenly heard the mother shouting. "My baby!" I broke down. My body was breaking down as I released freezing cold tears that rolled down my cheeks, one-by-one. I had met eye to eye with this little girl and my faith in humanity had been restored. If I could stand here holding a stranger in my arms, in a rage but at the ready to fight for her well-being, there were others who would do exactly the same. I wasn't alone. I was certain of that.

"Give me my baby!" I broke down once again but this time I was confronted with an angry mother. She snatched the baby from my arms as she frantically snapped at me in her mother tongue. Her husband put his arm around her shoulders and guided her away from me. She snuggled her head on his chest. He put his hand over his daughter's belly whilst her mother held her tight. So tight. Even tighter than I had been holding her just a couple of seconds ago. "Just a couple of seconds ago," I thought to myself. I admired the couple as I watched them walk away. Perhaps admire isn't the right word, but I truly did admire their strength. I had judged them when I caught the sight of them taking a selfie. I found it extraordinary to have 'forgotten' about their child once they had reached a foreign land. But in their own naivety they had 'made it'. They had crossed the shores into Europe. They had got their 'money's worth'. They had disembarked from their worst nightmare. And they were here, within my realms. Realms which

I knew would never meet their expectations. And if they eventually did reach their expectations, I knew that they would carry the very same nostalgia I had about a place called 'home'. There was no ending to this course.

"There are another five boats crossing the sea. What do you want to do? Shall we stay here a little longer or do you want to go? I've got some great shots," murmured Arthur after he had made his way to me holding his camera in his hands, zapping through his photos.

I couldn't speak. Tears continued to roll down my cheeks but this time Arthur caught the sight of them.

"Come on," he nodded sideways with his head. "It's time to go. Let me take you home. We'll make some nice soup. Put some warm dry clothes on." He grabbed me by the hand. I looked at him with all my might. I knew he was right. I fought against my resistance and took a step forward. I cried in silence all the way home. 'Home', I thought to myself. A bed in a tiny flat on the shores of Lesvos. Today that was my home. It was my home because I knew I would feel safe there. Safe. I recalled the little girl's eyes and I wished that she was safe. That her new home for tonight would, at the very least, make her feel safe.

Chapter 7

Parting

"The brokered EU-Turkey deal, which came into force this morning, is a statement of cooperation between European states and the Turkish government. It seeks to control the crossing of refugees and migrants from Turkey to the Greek islands, and was initially intended to curb the large numbers of refugees arriving in Europe – or losing their lives on the way – particularly in 2015. The crux of the deal was that every person arriving irregularly (i.e. by boat, without official permission or passage) to the Greek islands – including asylum-seekers – would be returned to Turkey. In exchange, EU Member States would take one refugee from Turkey for every refugee returned from the islands."

I had taken the 'day off' from the camp in order to attempt to report back to Cyprus about the situation on the ground. I sat on the terrace of a picturesque little harbour just over half an hour away from the camp, with my laptop, facing the sea. I was seeking fresh air, the vast view of the sea, an alternative environment from the one I had found myself in for the past month or so.

Oliver had spontaneously got in touch with me and had asked me to write 'something'; a 'news feature' he said, a piece that would give the essence of what was happening on the ground. The more I wrote, the more I deleted, the more I deleted the more I realised I was incapable of depicting reality. There were so many angles from which to address the situation, and none of them rang true. Not enough words could ever mirror the truth and merely stating the facts didn't appeal to me. Perhaps that was why I was so discouraged by media reports. I didn't want to spread fear but it seemed that whichever way I approached things, fear was at the helm. Even the word *sea* seemed to have a different connotation nowadays. Refugees crossed the sea, drowned in the sea, feared the sea themselves, smugglers abused the sea, flaunted it, it was the sea that divided 'us' from 'them', it was the sea that carried people on the move, let them down at times; in so many ways, it was the sea who regulated the movement of peoples.

I picked up the phone. After a couple of rings I heard Oliver's voice.

"Hi Oliver, it's Christine," I hesitantly said as I looked out at sea.

"You got something for me?" he answered, never minding how I was.

"Euh, no," I replied after a long silence.

"So why are you calling me? You're wasting my time."

"Please, please Oliver, don't hang up. You don't understand. I'm coming back home tonight and I'm really trying to get my head around things here. I can't report back, not as a news piece..."

"Did you speak to the mayor? The head of UNHCR? The police?" He wasn't interested in what I was trying to tell him.

"Yes, yes, I've spoken to them. I told you I would. Their facts are one-sided and they have nothing to say about the lives of people being ripped to pieces. They're focused on the EU-Turkey agreement right now, that's all they talk about, or hide behind," I reflected holding my forehead in my right hand. "And every time I prod at any humanity, they talk off the record. No one will talk to me about the violation of human rights, about the health hazards, about how they would feel should they find themselves in an equivalent situation."

"Feel? I'm not interested in feelings Christine. You work for a newspaper for God's sake, not a glossy magazine," he laughed. "I want something that sells. Talk to me about the EU-Turkey agreement. Talk to me about the closing of the Macedonian border and how that will stop refugees from making their way into Central Europe. That 'Balkan Route' you always talk about. It doesn't seem that appealing anymore does it?" he chuckled again.

"But don't you get it? Even if the Macedonian border is closing down, people will still find one way or another to get into Europe, it's not going to change the root of the problem. I don't care about any EU-

Turkey agreement. Turkey's making millions of euros on the back of people's lives, never mind them
using this agreement as a political bait... People are
suffering Oliver," I took in a deep breath. I knew I
was shooting myself in the foot. He would never re-
gard me as a journalist anymore. Not that he ever
really did.

"I'm sorry Oliver, I need to put my foot down here.
But what I was really calling you about was to ask you
whether I could write a piece in the first person. A
column perhaps, to denote my experience, as Christine, not as a journalist." I cringed as I awaited for his
answer. I was ready to be shut down.

"Whatever. Do whatever you think Christine; as
long as you have good photos to dress the article
with. Photos sell. I'm not really interested in how
you see things or how you feel, but I'm sure we can
use your piece as a filler at some point. Christmas is
coming up. We always struggle for content at Christmas. Talk to you when you get back." The phone line
went dead.

"Filler," I thought to myself. "Typical." I looked at
my computer screen and the content of the first
paragraph of the news article I had been attempting
to write just before I had reached out for my phone
to call Oliver. Letter by letter I deleted every single
word I had written by repeatedly pressing down
hard on the backspace key of my keyboard. It was
almost therapeutic.

"What would you like to eat?" asked an older looking man who was wearing a dark green beanie. Right. Food. Not a commodity I thought of often these days but I missed fish. And salad.

"Are you a fisherman?" I had seen him fiddle with fishing nets just across from where I was sitting, aside a fishing boat named 'Hope'.

"Yes! I'm the owner of this place and a fisherman," he smiled as he proudly looked around and eventually grabbed the back of the chair next to me. He leaned forward over the chair. He really did look like a typical fisherman. His beanie, his olive green woolly jumper. His wellies. I smiled back at him. It was refreshing to see someone make a living out of his passion.

"Well maybe you can tell me what fish I should eat then. Do you have any fresh fish of the day?" I queried. He took some time to examine me and then he looked out at sea. It took him a couple of seconds to find the words to respond. I wondered what was happening in his mind.

"I've got fresh fish. From this morning. But let me tell you young lady," he paused again, as if in some kind of agony, "I don't eat the fish I catch," he eventually blurted out, "or any fish that comes from our shores for that matter."

"What? Why?" I twisted in my chair and faced him head on.

"Because the fish is contaminated. It's dirty. It's inedible." He carried on gazing out at sea as though he was begging its pardon. Still contemplating, he carried on talking. I half-heartedly listened; I wasn't prepared to delve into any other kind of misery.

"For years now, the Italians have been dumping their nuclear waste in our seas, all over Greece and around its islands, right in the middle of the Mediterranean and our fish are being singed by it. They live off that shit!"

"Are you sure about this? Surely this can't be entirely true. Greece would never let this be," I was dumbfounded but alert. I even thought of calling Oliver. He would be all over this story. But then I remembered where I was and why I was here. I looked down at the concrete floor anticipating my next move.

"Italy is paying Greece to get rid of its waste in Greek waters! And now, with the crisis, what easier way to make quick money? Hm? Can't you see? Politicians are willingly killing our eco systems in the name of money. Not power. Money. And you know what the worst thing about it is?"

"Look, I'm sorry to interrupt you but I need to go," I stood up looking for my purse in my bag. "Thank you for the coffee. It's a lovely place you have here..." I needed to walk away from this. Erase it from my mind altogether, if ever possible. I literally couldn't handle the information. I handed him a five euro note.

He refused my money.

"Coffee's on me, I'm sorry if I unsettled you, I was just…"

"No, no, no need to apologise, it's all a little too much for me. I'll come back another time. Have a good day sir!" I turned away and legged it to my car. I drove straight back to the camp. I had enough to deal with. I couldn't get involved in the fisherman's story. There might have been no truth to his story but it did play on my mind. It was my last day on the island and I wanted to say goodbye to so many people.

I walked around the camp all afternoon. I now knew it like the back of my hand. I knew every stone, every tent, every washing line, every tree. At the central part of the camp, where the soup tent, the clothes tent and the children's tent were set up in a semi-circle, lots of people had gathered, volunteers and refugees talked amongst themselves, some chopped vegetables, others handed out clothes, dealt with the rubbish, hung out clothes to dry, others just sat on the ground. Hopeless. Useless. Killing time. I watched the busyness in melancholy. As extraordinary as it sounded, I was going to miss this place. This raw reality. I walked a little further down. A new tent had been set up. I wanted to say hello. At the entrance of the black and red tent was a carpet with a little baby sitting amongst rucksacks, propped up by a pile of dry clothes. She must have been no more than 9 or ten months old. She wore a pink headband over her little ears. And there she sat, all alone. There was a red balloon floating above her, tied to the tent, a sign that her parents had taken her to the children's tent. In the children's tent, volunteers gave balloons out to every child who came to spend some time with them. I approached her as I looked around for her parents, or siblings. It was unusual to see children on their own in the camp. There was no one in the proximity though. I ducked down towards her.

"Hey there, little one. What are you doing here sitting in the middle of this big carpet?" I smiled. Not that I was anticipating any reply from her, I merely responded to her being. She looked so calm. Content. She was holding something in her hand but I couldn't see what it was.

"Hey, Christine, I've been looking for you!" It was Arthur.

"I'll drive with you to the airport, I don't want you to drive out there all alone. We can drop the rental car off at the rental office together and then I'll find my way back. No worries."

I stood up and gave him a hug. That said it all. I had had a lump in my throat since that morning and his coming with me somewhat alleviated my sorrow. I really didn't want to drive to the airport alone.

"Thank you. Thank you so much," I whispered in his ear as I held him in my embrace. "I'll meet you at the flat in a couple of hours. I'll be ready." I waved to him as I turned to get closer to the little girl once again. That's when I saw a yellow piece of something in her mouth.

"What the hell is that?" I thought to myself. I pulled my hand out of my pocket to reach for her mouth but I suddenly felt conscious. Self-conscious. What was I doing putting my fingers in a baby's mouth? A stranger's mouth. I was worried about someone seeing me. Judging me. Not understanding what it was I was doing. I looked to the left and then to the right. No one was minding me. "Fuck it." I reached out my index finger into her tiny mouth only to re- alise there was something that felt like thin plastic at the back of her throat. She seemed to be breath- ing but I panicked. The potential of her choking on whatever was in her mouth was imminent. I grabbed the back of her head, cupping it in my hand and with my thumb and index finger I pushed my way into her mouth until I felt I had got a hold of something. Out I pulled the tying knot of a yellow balloon. "Je- sus," I thought to myself. I looked at the little girl who was now quite happily lying on my crossed legs, my hand still cupped behind her head, providing her with a comfortable cushion. I looked for her par- ents. I looked for her siblings. But there was no one. I wanted to go the children's tent to alarm them, tell them that giving out balloons wasn't such a good idea after all. I waited. I even contemplated taking her home with me. I was so relieved when her mom appeared out of nowhere.

"Shoukran, shoukran," she said to me. "Milk," she pointed at the baby bottle she was holding in her hands. It had obviously taken her a while to find some. Little did she know her daughter had almost choked to death as she waited for her. I kissed the little girl on her forehead, passed her on to her mother and waved goodbye to the family. The father had arrived with another three boys. I walked away considering my departure. How all of us played so many different roles here, how we just got along with things as they happened. How we forgot about how much we achieved every single day, even though we felt we never did quite enough.

Night was slowly falling and I could feel my departure was approaching. Time wasn't on my side anymore. I hadn't even packed my bags. I needed to go. I made my way to the car with my eyes wide open. I looked at every face that walked past me and made sure I said goodbye to each and everyone of them. And for each of them I wished that they would stay safe; refugees and volunteers alike. That they would find their way. Somehow.

As I stepped onto the tarmac road, I clicked on the car keys and my emergency lights blinked twice in the distance. I was heading straight for the car when all of a sudden a tall man walked straight up to me and grabbed me by the shoulders. He must have been three heads taller than me; very slim and he wore a black turban on his head. His cheeks dipped into his cheek bones. His eyes where dark and murky. His lips were chapped. I got such a fright.

"Is Germany full?" He spoke loud and clear, held my shoulders tight in his hands and looked at both of my eyes, one by one, from one to the other, in search of a response.

I broke away from his stare and looked down at my feet. Once I grasped the courage to look back up at him again, I asked him what his name was.

"Mohammed," he answered, still holding on to my shoulders but not that tight anymore.

"I'm sorry Mohammed. Of course Germany isn't full. It can never be full. Do you understand me?" I looked for his eyes for he was now looking at the ground. "Despair," I thought to myself.

"I want to go home," he shook his head. "I want to go home," he sat on the ground.

"It's alright Mohammed, it's alright," I put my arm over his shoulder as we both sat on the wet ground next to each other. "You'll find your way. Don't cry, you'll find your way," I tried to reassure him. Was I lying again? I sat there with him for another half hour or so until I led him to the soup tent. There I introduced him to Ralph and Elena. He would be in good hands. I had to go.

Once on the plane I looked down at the streetlights shining on the coast of Lesvos. I don't think I've ever cried so much on an aeroplane. I often cried on aeroplanes for I hated goodbyes. But this was different of course. I opened my laptop along with an empty word document. I began to write. For the newspaper. To Oliver. To Dara. To my family. To my friends. To the world. To whoever was willing to listen:

'Lesvos. December 2015. I'm standing on a hill

next to the official refugee registration camp of the island. On average, there are 700 refugees making their way to us, per day. It's pouring with rain. The bin bag I'm wearing over my shoulders doesn't really make do. Neither do my means.

A family of five all need dry clothes. And shoes. A man travels alone carrying a plastic bin bag filled with his belongings over his shoulder. A little girl holds her guardian's hand. She looks tired. Cold. Hungry. Hundreds of people walk up the hill in a deafening silence. Having just entered Europe, most of their journeys have been extensively long. Yet, it's still the beginning; onwards they tread towards an unknown destination, an ambiguous process, a failed humanity, perhaps.

I try to determine their nationality, their needs; their anguish. What's your name? Are you cold? How long have you been travelling? Did you get a registration ticket? What's your number? How many of you are travelling together? Is there a baby travelling with you? Where are you heading?

As European policies violate human rights and move further and further away from any kind of humane approach to the constant movements of peoples, it is solely when I look back at distinct moments while working on the Better Days for Moria Refugee Camp that my ultimate frustration is replaced by an overwhelming tenderness, a woven basket, if you like, filled with emotions of all sorts: joy, sadness, frustration, satisfaction, endurance, hopelessness, dignity, shame...

You see, it's easy to try and build an idea about what it's like out there. The photos the media floods us with are pretty much self-articulate. We have had children drown on our shores. But how can I convey the feeling of Wida's embrace after she mimed the loss of her family of 8, while on the 2-year journey that eventually led her into my arms?

How can I forget 3-year-old Amir's sneaky little smile after he proudly slipped on a pair of a size 25, brand new, blue and orange Adidas train-ers, which he refused to take off, even though they were a size too small for him?

How can I still not find the correct echo to re-spond to Mohammed's implausible question: "Is Germany full?"

These notions, however, may lend a hand to ex-plaining why time stood still in Moria. Daily life there was unpredictable. Visions were hard to re-alise, the sole reason being that realities changed by the hour, events happened by the minute, needs rarely ceased to exist.

Yet it is also within this physically demanding, internal turmoil that the purest form of human-ity exudes its potentials. This was clear when, every morning, a group of refugees would whole-heartedly join me to collect the countless empty paper cups and water bottles that had relieved their hunger and thirst. None of us would shy away from lifting the dozens of silver and golden hypothermia blankets that only recalled the uncertain sea journey each and every refugee had taken across the sea. Hanging countless wet clothes left behind after being exchanged for dry ones, was a mechanical duty that only emphasised the number of people that passed through these premises day in, day out.

On a sunny afternoon, a young Afghan took the initiative and began helping a group of volunteers manning a tent that provided tea and soup on a 24-hour basis. He'd carried barrels of water to us from the running water tap at the top of the hill. By nightfall he stood proudly beside us and handed out bottles of water as we distributed cups of soup. Returning to serve breakfast early the next morning, Amir Rosey was already in place, ready to help, even before I had arrived. But this time, he wasn't alone. I smiled at the lady standing next to him as we realised we were the same age. Little did I know it was Amir Rosey's mother. Her name was Wesa and she was 35. Amir Rosey was 22.

In the tent, Wesa sang Afghan songs as she chopped garlic for the Afghan soup we were preparing for the camp. I can't describe the awe I felt as a translator transmitted Wesa's joy. She was so happy to be cooking. Having left her daughter and husband behind in Kabul, she hadn't got her hands 'dirty' for the past two months. For a moment there, she found purpose. For a moment there, Wesa felt human again.

That was the moment I accepted the beauty of the short-term nature of our offerings and ceased to look at the wider picture. Imprinted in my soul are moments of pure coexistence, where the very present abolishes the tragedy of the camp's reality and induces a distinct compassion for one another that I had, up until then, never really experienced at first hand.

Somewhere here is also where I completely grasped the core notion of volunteerism. This is where I began treasuring the sheer exchange that is provided through reaching out to people in need. A lot of our work stemmed from communicating with refugees along with providing the very basic: food, water, warm clothes, toothbrushes, underwear. Yet I was also recurrently reminded about how far compassion can go, how much a smile or an embrace can lend to someone's unimaginable journey, how spending time with little children relieved the mothers' anguish for a while, how life in the camp was all about functioning on a purely human, intuitive level. We all needed and we all need each other in order to make a difference.

It is also here where I encountered how a group of dedicated, selfless individuals independently *strove to work alongside the Greek State and official NGOs who could only operate within government premises.*

Within the official camp, the Greek State, UN-HCR, Mercy Worldwide and other NGOs, such as Action Aid and Save the Children focused on providing aid for Syrian refugees because that was the initial influx.

But eventually, as many of you will know, there were also thousands of people coming from other countries, countries such as Afghanistan, Iran, Gambia and Pakistan, who didn't get any sort of humanitarian aid. These people were left without any guidance, without any health care, on their own, in a privately-owned field, on a hill, a place we initially called the Afghan hill, a place we referred to as the 'outside', a place we eventually named 'Better Days for Moria' because truly, that was our aspiration.

Assisting these people from the 'outside', without the proper infrastructure, guidance, means and ever-changing procedures and policies was, needless to say, challenging. Because most of us were inexperienced and learning as we went along, because once money began to flow in, coordination and vision became crucial. Being 'shut out' from official boundaries was infuriating, for as much as I can understand the logic behind maintaining a single authority to lead the way, the truth was that the help provided from the 'inside' wasn't enough.

Taking into account the immensity of the problem I'm addressing, drawing lines between migrants, economic migrants and refugees may have some logic from afar, but once on location, defining whom to help and whom to turn a blind eye to was not, and should not be an option.

On my last night, I waved goodbye to Mohammed as he boarded the ferry taking him to Athens. After almost two years, I was witnessing Mohammed's sheer drive to make his way to Germany after his father and brother had been shot in front of his eyes. Sitting by the campfire before making our way to the marina, I had hinted at the reality that the borders were closing down and that his passage was uncertain. His sheer glance told me that there was no going back for him. He was moving ahead. We pulled out some money to help him. At first he accepted it, but he quickly refrained from taking it. He pointed at a tent below us and told me the story of the family sleeping inside. Mother, father and four children under the age of eight had been living in that tent indefinitely due to the lack of 60 euros per person needed to board the ferry to Athens. He preferred we give them the money, but we insisted and agreed to give half to him and half to the family. This fairness gained ground and as we parted he made sure I knew that his appreciation for me, for all the volunteers, wasn't about the money, but about our hearts. I was overcome by his courage, his righteousness, his serenity and compassion for the other, regardless of the path he was handed. What an example to find amidst goodbyes.

I often look at the photo I took of Mohammed as we parted, and on many occasions I think of the journey he has made. As many of you will know, The 'Balkan Route' as we call it, the route that has led so many refugees across Europe is now closed. The Better Days for Moria Refugee Camp, as we speak, is also shutting down. The camp is being forced to close down under new legislation imposed by the European Union. Having said that, Mohammed may be one of the lucky ones who actually managed to reach his final destination. Very soon, Moria will be turned into a detention centre, a prison filled with souls who have lost hope for the future.

How governments will deal with displaced peoples left in limbo, whether in reception centres, camps, detention camps, at the Macedonia borders or any other border remains to be seen. But what we have to acknowledge is that, currently, there are some thousands of refugees who are making Europe their home and who are very much part of our future generation. They are here to stay.

I sometimes envisage the possibility of Amir becoming my daughter's classmate at University one day. You may laugh, but this is possible! To this end, what I personally need to make sure of, before this happens, is that my daughter understands and becomes very much aware of Amir's journey. And that Amir finds a balanced place within our realms, even if he wears a brand new pair of Adidas trainers!

I want to believe that most of you would agree that the complexity of the issue I'm addressing is overwhelming and that the first step that has to be taken in order to solve it, is to end our wars. But in the meantime, while policies are being revisited, our human values can still be at play. Quite precisely, I believe that it is perhaps one of the only means we have to make a difference.

Leaving Mytilini airport I instinctively bought myself a souvenir. A green lighter with 'I (heart) Lesvos' inscribed on one side. I never buy souvenirs when travelling. Yet it made sense this time around. I needed something to remind me of the raw reality I had now become part of. I needed a means to carry every single notion, person, vision, despair, truth and hope back with me; to make sure that my reality check back home was one that would urge me to continue to reach out to people in need. Because solidarity is the only way forward and because life as we know it today is not coherent with our core human values.[4]

Just before landing in Cyprus, I attached the word document in an e-mail to Oliver. I didn't care if he didn't like it. I didn't care if it wasn't what he was looking for. This was my truth. I pressed 'send'. I

[4] TEDx Talk, 'I'm not a volunteer, I'm human' Tedx Nicosia, 2016

closed my laptop. I disembarked amongst the over-whelming Christmas decorations of the Larnaca International Airport. The lights, the rush, the cleanliness and order of the premises made me feel sick. I messaged Dara, the only person I felt obliged to pretend I was alright to.

Hey my love, I've just landed. I'll be home as soon as I can. I miss you terribly, I changed paragraph. *Can't wait to hear your news*. I was lying. All I wanted to do was hide in a corner somewhere. I had no idea what my next steps were to be, neither did I really care. In all honesty, I had left my heart back on the shores of Lesvos, where people knew what it meant to be alive, in every sense of the word.

Chapter 8

Alternate Dimension

"You can't do that Christine, you're comparing this reality with the one you've just returned from and it's just not fair on Dara. It's Christmas, she'll never understand why you're being so rigid."

I was having a morning coffee with my mom before heading back to the newsroom for the first time since I'd returned from Lesvos. I was trying to forbid her from buying Christmas presents for Dara.

"She'll only get *one* Christmas present from me this year. No more," I'd clumsily instructed her. I'd emptied all my cupboards at home, given everything I considered I didn't need away to charity: clothes, books, kitchenware, even furniture. I had become radical in my ways. I couldn't bare to walk into supermarkets, I cursed people lingering around the aisles with shopping trolleys filled with stuff I reckoned they didn't need.

"There are people out there who have nothing to their name mom. It won't hurt Dara if she isn't spoilt for a year, she'll understand where I'm coming from. I think you're making too much of a deal out of this."

"*I'm* making too much of a deal? You were handed a different deck of cards in life Christine, don't deny that. You should feel grateful. Embrace it, come on my love, take it easy."

It wasn't the first time I felt misunderstood. My principles didn't seem to match my surroundings anymore.

An hour later, I walked into the office as if I had never left. I huffed at my empty coffee cup standing beside my computer screen. I put my bag down. As I turned to take my jacket off, a bunch of flowers appeared in my vision. The editorial team in the newsroom had decided to surprise me; welcome me 'home'. I was touched and moved to my core. I found it difficult to hold the tears back. We spent the next hour or so sharing notes. I began telling them about my journey. As I recounted my steps I felt as if it was all a dream and unexpectedly, I felt as if I was having a soft landing here; I had a 'family' waiting for me after all. As we mused about politics — it was unavoidable not to do so within the newsroom — Oliver walked through the door. I was nervous about seeing him.

"Here comes the humanitarian," he chuckled. "Hope you like the flowers. Come in my office when you're ready." He dropped some mail off on my desk and made his way to his office. Everyone looked at him silently and then turned back to me.

"I don't know if that's a good thing or a bad thing," I shrugged, turning toward the team now sitting comfortably around my desk. "Thanks for the flowers anyway, you shouldn't have, I'll keep them on my desk, might bring some colour into this place."

I sat at my desk staring at the computer screen as hundreds of emails downloaded into my inbox. I probably appeared busy but in truth I was wondering when a good time to walk into Oliver's office would be. Or what I was to expect. I felt on the edge with him at the best of times. I wasn't sure how I'd react if he rubbed me up the wrong way and I was suspecting he might. I plucked up the courage. I grabbed my coffee cup and made my way to his office door.

"I'm going in," I announced to everyone in the newsroom. Everybody nodded. All I heard was the blaring voice of the radio presenter coming from the radio across the room: "At least one person has died after a fire broke out at an overcrowded refugee camp on the Greek island of Lesvos, local officials say..."

I closed my eyes shut as I held on to the door handle tightly.

"They say the charred body of a woman was found at Moria camp. But unconfirmed reports say there was another victim, a child," the voice continued. My body froze. I couldn't move.

"Police fired teargas against protesting migrants who said fire-fighters were too slow to respond to the blaze. The camp houses about 12,000 people in tents and shipping containers." I let go of the door handle and attempted to make steps back to my desk. The radio presenter was talking about the official registration camp adjacent to the camp I knew so well. I wanted to call Arthur who was still there.

"Who's there?" I heard Oliver call out from inside his office.

"Shit," I thought to myself. "It's me Oliver," I opened the door. "Is this a good time?" I asked popping my head in through the door.

"Yeah, come in. Close the door behind you." I felt as though I was closing the door to Lesvos, to the camp, to all the faces I left behind. It pained me to move forward. I stepped into Oliver's office as if I was entering a time warp.

Oliver sat at his desk without saying a word. He was looking at his computer screen holding on to his mouse in his right hand, his chin was tucked into his neck making space for his eyes to see the screen over his eyeglasses. I waited. My patience astounded me.

After some time he finally looked up from his screen, took his glasses off and placed them aside his mouse.

"I'm going to run your piece. Next week. With your by-line. It's a courageous piece. You actually managed to move me. That says a lot doesn't it?" he chuckled.

"Don't let this go to your head," he continued, leaving me with no room to respond. "The newsroom's been suffering without your presence. I want you to cover a couple of extra shifts in the next couple of weeks. Relieve the others for a bit... what's your plan anyway? You staying with us?"

I had considered the possibility of leaving the newspaper before I had left for Greece. In a moment of a heated debate and fury, I had announced that I would call it quits. But I hadn't given it much more thought whilst I was away, even though I knew my time doing hard news was somewhat over.

"Well, euh, thank you. I mean, I don't know. How many shifts are you talking about? Are you running the piece in the Sunday paper?" I was asking way too many questions in one sentence. I was flustered. I didn't know where to start from. I shook my head from side to side.

"Let me start again," I proposed as I pulled out a chair to sit down and gather my thoughts. "I want to run interviews with refugees, here, in Cyprus." I took the plunge. "I want to write their stories in an attempt to shed light on why people opt to leave their homes and countries. Raise awareness about their journeys and experiences in hosting countries. I want to start with that, and eventually perhaps they will be able to find their own voice, speak for themselves, but at the moment I feel that they need other people to be their voice, they need help in telling their stories and getting people to hear them out, change people's perceptions perhaps. Only then will their hearts soften." It was in mid-sentence that I realised everything I was saying was probably way too soppy for Oliver. I had forgotten who I was talking to.

"There's an event. Tonight. They're calling it 'Sharing is Caring' or some crap. They're making food for the needy or whatever. You know, the hippy types.

Go there. Start with that," Oliver joked as he began to shuffle paper around on his desk. He'd broken eye contact with me. I knew this conversation was pretty much over. "Tomorrow you focus on the Cyprus peace talks; the President is departing for Berlin tomorrow morning where he will meet the Turkish Cypriot leader and the UN Secretary-General. They're hoping to restart the peace talks; not sure if you're aware of that," he smirked.

He annoyed me so much. "Yes, I know Oliver, I haven't been completely off the plot. Let me remind you that I *can* read; everyone's talking about it. It's the headline of every bloody news channel in Cyprus this morning!"

"Don't get hissy with me!" Oliver stood up. I crossed a line he wasn't willing to let go of. "Now move your cute little ass out of my office and sit it down to work. Enough of your prancing around. Earth calling Christine. Over and out." He sat back down again.

After a long silence I stood up and placed the chair back where I had found it.

"I'd appreciate it if you left my ass, as you so eloquently call it, *alone*!" I had walked up to his desk and we now found each other almost nose to nose. I shrugged my shoulders. "I haven't missed this place one bit. *One bit!*" I went to turn around to leave the room but then I opted not to. I stood tall in front of his desk once more. "You would never dare to talk to me like that if you were bringing up four daughters!"

I clenched my teeth. I almost carried on talking but just pressed on my jaw a little harder. I shuffled to the door and slammed it in full force stomping back to my desk. I cringed at the thought of my last sentence. I was such a child sometimes. Once back at my office, I found a piece of paper with a written message placed on my keyboard. "Don't watch the news. Your camp's on fire. We love you. xxx"

I was raging inside. I began to filter through my emails until Oliver's name popped up. I clicked on his email: *Here is the presser about the Caring event thing tonight. So you have it. You're a great journalist. C.*

I clicked on the attachment. "What an asshole," I thought to myself. I breathed out heavily. I felt the entire newsroom turn towards me to check on me. Grand entrance I was making for myself... *"Christmas dinner offered to the homeless, the needy and refugees. Setting up at 5pm, dinner served from 6.30 - 8.30pm. Come and help to set up, serve, and/or clear up. Some help also needed with cooking. And spread the word to those in need."*

"Christine. Christine? Your phone's ringing." Annie, who religiously sat next to me on late night shifts, was nudging me out of my daydream. Staring blankly at my computer screen, I was still contemplating on calling Arthur.

"Oh! Thanks. Sorry. I was distracted. Hello?" I answered the phone. My phone had ceased on being an extension to my arm while in the camp. I'd got out of the habit of seeking it. Even its ring tone sounded foreign.

"Hey girl! I know you've just got back but I'm going to this event tonight. Thought you'd like to join me. We're all cooking different things and gathering in the municipal market to try and make a Christmassy dinner for refugees and the homeless. You know? The old municipal market down town? Everything's ready, you don't have to bring anything if you haven't got the time, but I was wondering if you could help us out with some final logistics."

Marcia had been a friend of mine for over ten years. Always as direct, but she knew me well. Never cut round corners when it came to important matters.

"Logistics?"

"Well we're looking for tables and chairs. So that people can have a proper sit down dinner, we want to decorate the tables and bring a real Christmas spirit, you know?"

I hadn't been back in the office for 24 hours yet and my mind was already flooded with information.

"Tell me what you need Marcia," I said bluntly.

"Someone mentioned that the UN could help us with tables and chairs. Apparently they've helped other events in the past. And they have the trucks to trans-port the tables and chairs and everything. I thought maybe you have a contact there, you know, with all the stuff you write about them, you must know someone who can direct us to the right person?"

"The UN's meeting with the President in Berlin tomorrow," I answered pointlessly.

"What?"

"Nothing. Forget it. Let me think about it. I'll text you."

"You sure you're alright?"

"Yeah, yeah, no worries. I'll see you tonight in any case. Speak to you later."

More emails. More headlines. More bad news. I edited a couple more news stories and decided to call it a day. I was determined to get to the municipal market to see if my contact had worked. I also wanted to get a feel of what was happening on the ground. I wondered if there would be many refugees there. Just before I had departed for Lesvos I had witnessed someone living on the streets for the first time since I had moved to the island. Never in the 20 years that I had lived in Nicosia had I come across anyone making the streets their home.

I reached the municipal market within the old town of Nicosia about an hour before the event was to start. To my delight, a dozen UN soldiers were unloading folding tables and chairs and taking them into the market.

"Have you got a sticker?" asked a stranger at the door of the market. I looked at her confused.

"All volunteers need to write their name on a sticker and stick it on their chest. There's a lot of us and it will be easier for us to work like that," she added, handing me a blank sticker and a marker pen.

"Thanks," I smiled. This seemed so advanced in comparison to the camp. Markers and stickers seemed like a luxury; a good idea in any case. I walked into the market hesitantly. Dozens of people were busy doing different things. Food was coming in big metal trays, cutlery was being wrapped in fancy, colourful paper napkins, the tables where being set with paper plates and silvery knives and forks, there was even a table filled with presents for children wrapped in colourful Christmas wrapping paper. Donated toys from what I was told. I felt so much at home all of a sudden. It warmed my heart being amongst all these people working towards a common goal. Everyone was cheerful. Everything had meaning.

"Excuse me," I heard a man's voice coming from behind me. I turned abruptly.

"Hi," I said in exclamation. I was standing in front of an extremely handsome black, middle-aged man. He was dressed in dark jeans and a V-necked burgundy jumper with a light grey shirt. For a minute I wasn't sure who I was talking to. I wondered if he was a volunteer or someone attending the event. He looked too smart and composed for a refugee, yet too seemingly lost to be a local.

"Where did you get your name tag from?" he asked politely. He was so subtle in his being it was enchanting.

"Oh! You're a volunteer!" I assumed. "There's a lady passing them around, she was at the door a couple of minutes ago," I lifted my chin up and stood on my tiptoes looking for her.

"A volunteer," he said, bringing me back to the soles of my feet. "I'm an asylum seeker but I want to be a volunteer, I mean I want to help," he continued as steady as a monk.

His attitude was charming.

"The more the merrier," I chuckled, not knowing what to say. I was blushing and it made me feel uncomfortable.

"Where are you from?" he asked me. "You don't look Cypriot."

"Ah, yes, people say that to me all the time," I spoke slowly, as if I was trying to gain time. "I'm from Belgium but I've lived most of my life in Cyprus. You?"

"Cameroon," he smiled. "The English part of Cameroon as you probably gathered, but I speak some French. Tu es belle," he sneakily added.

"There's the lady!" I pointed across the room, ignoring his comment. His words had taken me out of my comfort zone. It had been a while since a man had flirted with me. I was adamant that men in Cyprus didn't know how to flirt. And up until that day it never occurred to me that a refugee or an asylum seeker would flirt with me. As if any kind of sexual promiscuity was forbidden when life took you astray to a strand of society different from the one you're used to. I waved at the sticker lady in an attempt to draw her closer to us and began walking to meet her half way. "She's got the stickers," I turned to him, realising I didn't know his name.

"I'm Christine," I stretched my arm out.

"Beni," he replied. He bowed a little as he accepted my hand in a handshake. I introduced Beni to the sticker lady and moved away from them seeking to make myself useful. I walked by a massive metal rocking horse in the centre of the market. Dozens of children were trying to climb and sit on it as it rocked back and forth. People across the room had started serving themselves food. The long stretch of tables was now animated with people sitting on either side. I wondered how many nationalities were gathered in the room. What their individual stories were. How they all made their way to Cyprus.

My daydream found me sitting on a chair next to a column almost in the centre of the room. I sat in contemplation as I watched a group of musicians setting up to play Christmas carols for the evening. Five of them wore red and white velvety Santa hats and another four wore reindeer antler headbands on their heads. I chuckled at the sight of them. "Pretentious," I thought to myself. I recalled a group of clowns who had made their way to the camp. For an entire morning they had managed to bring laughter to the place. We had clapped and cheered as their goo-goo eyes and multi-coloured outfits evoked our inner child.

"Do you want a beer?" Beni appeared out of nowhere and stood tall beside me, holding a plastic pint cup in his hands. He smiled holding it up in front of me.

"Sure! Let me get it. Do you want a refill?"

"Let me get it," he grabbed my arm as I stood up.

"No, no, it's on me, it's on me, no arguing," I pulled away. "I'll be right back." My motive was none other than to spare him any expenditure that didn't have to do with his necessities. I even questioned where he got money to buy himself beer. I dismissed his chivalry in the name of his status. His predisposition spoke to me more than his actual being.

"Do you smoke?" I asked, handing him his pint of beer. I searched for my cigarettes in my bag but realised I had none.

"You smoke?" he answered, surprised.

"Well, I've run out. Do you mind walking to the kiosk?"

We both wrapped ourselves in our jackets and scarfs and made our way through to the pedestrian side streets that wove through the old town. We didn't stop talking until we reached the kiosk. He recounted how happy he was to have made it to the event and how he had found out about it. He touched on his relatively recent arrival on the island, we talked about the civil war in Cameroon which he pinpointed as the final straw for his departure. The civil war had turned his life into a living nightmare. He estimated that there was no future there as a thirty something year old. The phone lines had been cut off since he had taken a flight out three weeks ago and he hadn't been able to get in touch with any of his family members, albeit through a connection he had who lived further away from the clashes and knew where his family lived. This man had promised him he would be in touch when and if he had any news, but he had had none.

"I just want my mom to know that I'm okay," he said as we made our way back to the market, cigarettes in hand. He looked down at the road as he spoke, and when he lifted his head up he tried to catch my eye. I was sure I knew what he was thinking. Or perhaps what he thought I was thinking. How could he leave his mother behind? I shrugged off my thoughts in certainty that we would meet again and have this conversation. It was the look in his eyes that told me he was seeking to share.

"What's this?" asked Beni walking into the market and pointing at a three by two white canvas draped from the ceiling.

"Do you want to draw something?" a young lady approached us with a set of multi-couloured pens in her hand. "One of you has to stand on this pedestal here, and tell the other what to draw. And then you swap."

Beni looked excited. I felt reluctant to engage, but we did.

"Could you take a photo of us?" Beni handed his phone to a passer-by.

"Give me your number," he then asked me, "I'll send you the photos."

We walked away laughing at our drawings. I was having fun with him yet I consciously kept my distance. I resisted for I knew our worlds were miles apart.

"Are you religious?" he whispered as I put my hands in my pockets making a standstill, admiring the Christmas carols, shying away from his closeness.

His question surprised me. I found it difficult to tell people who presumably came from religious backgrounds that my faith isn't embedded in a specific religion as such. As if prying into my beliefs affirmed what kind of person I was.

"What?" I clumsily replied trying to avoid the question, or just trying to buy myself time.

"What I mean is: do you go to church?" he continued.

His second question somehow made it even more difficult for me to venture into explaining my stance.

"Well, yes, I guess I do. But not to the conventional church you're most probably thinking of. A church for me can be anywhere, it's a place you feel comfortable in, a place in which you can take the time to reflect and really think for yourself, for a certain period of time," I replied in the hope that I wouldn't offend him.

He nodded in agreement, yet seemingly unsatisfied with my answer, he continued to prod. "I see. So like your home?"

"Yes, if you like. Or nature. That's a big church for me," I added.

We got closer to the musicians playing. People gathered around us, took photos, smiled or just stood pensively just as Beni did. It's not the easiest thing to get into the Christmas spirit when you're far away from your loved ones; never mind when you're living on practically nothing and waiting for an answer whether the country you're trying to make a new home in will accept you in the community as a permanent resident, or not.

"I go to church," he added eventually, breaking my line of thought. "All my family does. Do you know the Catholic Church here in Nicosia?"

"Yes, of course," I replied shortly. "I like going there to listen to people sing, it's heart-warming," I answered. Beni turned towards the musicians who were now playing in full swing and fell in a long silence; I would have given anything to know what was going through his mind.

"There you are!" Marcia appeared out of nowhere. We hugged for what felt like an eternity. "I missed you so much," she whispered in my ear. "You sounded off on the phone earlier, are you sure you're alright?" she pulled back cupping my jaw with both her hands while inspecting my face.

"I'm fine," I shied away. "This is Beni," I turned to my side in an attempt to include him in the conversation. They chatted for a while. I watched them engage and contemplated how comfortable he was with himself. How well he managed his presumably heavy past. How we all had stories up our sleeves that we dressed up so well.

"We're going for a drink at that bar we met in before you left. Do you want to join us?" Marcia was in party mode. I had no urge to continue the night. I wanted to go home. Cuddle up in my bed. Revert to myself. In many ways I felt I'd over exposed myself. I felt vulnerable and unable to pick up the lifestyle I had left behind when I went to Lesvos.

"I want to go home honey, I'm not in the mood. We'll catch up another time," I explained to Marcia.

"You're leaving?" interrupted Beni. "Let's take a photo."

We made our way outside the market onto the market square where Beni pulled his cell phone out of his pocket to take a selfie of the three of us sitting on a bench. It was pitch dark but the streetlight shed an orangey light upon us. I felt we were marking the culmination of what was an important event for solidarity in Nicosia. We giggled as we peeled the mandarins we had been given on our way out. The artificial lighting of the square gave off a tone of colour that evoked the sunset, the mandarins offered a taste that belonged to the Christmas, wintry season. It reminded me of my dream about strawberries while I was on

Lesvos, but this time round the fruit itself reassured me that nature was indeed always there to nurture us with its fruit and energy. It was such a soothing moment.

After we parted from Marcia I offered to drive Beni home. The buses were few and far between and it was cold out there. Nothing was too far in Nicosia. In the car, he laughed at the fact that a woman was driving a car or, even more extraordinary, was driving him home. We discovered that our houses were actually very close to one another, that my neighbourhood was familiar to him because it was were the Social Services' office was located. As I parked outside his flat, he pulled out a little plastic figurine and offered it to me as a present.

"I found it on the floor in the market," he said. "It's not much but it's to say thank you for sharing the evening with me, I don't feel as alone as I did before going out tonight. Thank you." His gesture touched me. "I'll keep it here on my dashboard," I said. "Thank you."

I drove home with the thought that the weather was getting colder and wondered whether he had everything he needed to keep warm. I knew it was a struggle for asylum seekers to obtain anything close to luxury, even a thin blanket. Deep down I also knew that I would hear from him again. There was a certain connection between us which I wasn't sure what to make of. But I was curious to find out why he had suddenly appeared in my life.

Chapter 9

Beni's Reality

I woke up with five text messages from Beni. One was a photo of me drawing a red heart with the word 'Belgium' inscribed in its centre, loosely floating on the side of the massive white canvas in the market. The other one was a photo of both of us posing in front of the finished drawing, smiling at the camera, as if we had known each other for years. The following messages were a heart, a smiley face and the words *thanks for the ride*.

"Good morning. My pleasure. Anytime," was all I could answer. I was sitting on my veranda. I hadn't done this since the winter had really kicked in but the mornings still offered some soothing warmth. It was definitely warmer than what it had been on Lesvos. As I sipped a slightly sugared Greek coffee, my phone rang again.

> *I'm at the Social Insurance office near your house. They've lost my papers. The next bus is in an hour. This has been going on for a month.*

As blunt as his written words were, I knew this scenario only too well. It was almost as though the Social Insurance Service delayed paperwork on purpose. Most asylum seekers I talked to in Nicosia were in the same limbo. If they didn't register with Social Insurance Service they couldn't get food vouchers, a rent allowance, any prospect of a rental agreement and their interview with the asylum services was postponed; a bureaucracy that inhumanly controlled the processing of peoples on the move. In the meantime, homelessness increased, hunger triumphed and hopelessness swelled. Everything depended on registering with the Social Insurance Service and Beni was nowhere near. I hated the system but in the back of my mind I also knew that the situation was still much better than the one faced in the camp.

Nevertheless, I couldn't sit at ease. In a matter of minutes I got dressed and walked out the door.

I'm coming to pick you up. I'll take you to where you need to go. I'll meet you in the parking. Be there in 10'.

Outside the Social Insurance building there were a dozen people standing around on the pavement, seemingly waiting for something. Not a soul looked local; most were Africans who, I was aware, came here day in, day out, in the hope that someone would address their concern, address the paperwork that they had somehow managed to pull together; micromanage a slice of their personal story that revealed absolutely nothing when written in black and white.

Now parked in the parking lot, I looked around to see if I could spot him; all of a sudden I wasn't sure if

I would be able to recognise him in a different context from the previous night.

"He'll make his way to me," I thought to myself.

As I patted the passenger seat in an attempt to get rid of the lingering crumbs Dara had left behind while she had eaten her breakfast in the car, I noticed someone walking towards the car. Getting a closer look, it looked nothing like Beni. He looked so much younger. And he didn't look as smart as I remembered him; he wore a trendy dark blue hoodie over his head and loose baggy jeans and was holding a sports bag over his shoulder as though he was merely coming out of the gym. He got into my car, sat on the passenger seat and reached out for his seatbelt.

"Thanks for coming to get me," he said, his voice ringing familiar bells in my mind. Taken aback by his allure, I struggled to find my words. I mechanically pressed on the clutch and changed gear to neutral. Almost under my own breath, I murmured. "How did it go? Did you get anywhere?"

"No." He paused, turned towards me and looked at me as though he had seen me for the first time in his life. Breaking an uncomfortable silence he continued to talk: "They say they don't have my asylum application form, that I have to file a new one. I don't understand how they could lose my papers," he continued as a matter of fact.

I started the car in response to his frustration. I was crap at reacting to desperation.

"I'm sorry. This is easy to say but... patience. You can rely on patience." I was on the point of delivering a prep talk of some kind but I felt I didn't have the means.

"Will you come back and try again tomorrow?"

He didn't reply. He persisted in looking out of the car window.

Making our way towards the city, he explained how he recognised the surroundings seeing as he had taken the same route on the bus that very morning. I eventually also heard him speak broken French on the phone to his room mate who was from the French part of Cameroon. They spoke broken French together and I was surprised at how much I could understand, being a native French speaker.

Hanging up the phone, Beni laughed at how much I had understood from his conversation.

"I guess colonies pay off somehow!" he smiled. My Belgian roots often put me in an awkward position when mingling with people from particular African countries which had suffered in the name of my ancestors.

"Today I'm Cypriot," I laughed, trying to deflect the conversation. It occurred to me that I had no idea where we were going.

"It's getting cold at night and we can't seem to stay warm," he mused.

"Do you know of the NGO 'Caritas'? They're giving out blankets but it's been a couple of days since they put an announcement out, I want to see if they still have some blankets," he said, still gazing out of the car window. His gaze seemed to look right through the buildings that surrounded us, as though he was physically in the car but mentally elsewhere. I thought about one of the conversations we had had the previous night; about loneliness. Considering that he had fled his country alone and having a sound understanding of how lonely it can be to try and grow new roots in a foreign city, he had denied that he was lonely; he felt he was merely alone in his existence, that loneliness was something else.

"I can take you with the car if you want," I proposed. "I mean, how will you carry the blankets home?"

He smiled at the idea. I looked away. He stared out of the car window some more. The silence in the car had become unexpectedly comfortable. The day was young. The sun was high. I had every intention of reverting to my routine yet I wanted to spend some time with him. Get to know him a little bit more.

Once at the Caritas offices, we found two blankets. They reminded me of my childhood; thick woollen brown and beige blankets just like my grandmother used to have; so heavy, there was no need to be tucked in at night.

"All the stuff we have at home belongs to someone else," muttered Beni as he put the blankets in the boot of the car and hastily made his way to the passenger door. "Plates, pans, beds. Nothing is of our choice," he added as he sat in the car. I noticed some aggravation in his voice. He was implying something I couldn't latch on to.

"But it was your choice to come to Cyprus, no? I mean, you chose to leave your country?" I had asked him the same question the night before but somehow the daylight made it all the more real, almost demanding another kind of sincerity than the one expressed while holding a beer in our hands.

"Do you want to sit down and talk? I would love to get to know your mindset," answered Beni.

He had already mentioned my mindset a couple of times. I felt as if he wanted to tap into my thinking in order to make sense of the 'new world' he was now becoming part of. As if I could somehow convey my entire life experience to him and that with that knowledge he would have the power and confidence to move forward.

Tending to asylum seeker's needs often boiled down to practical needs: blankets, food, guidance in bureaucracy and merely an ear to listen. I often confronted that bridge between helping and becoming responsible for someone and in the process I was acquiring an ever increasing number of additional responsibilities. My return from Lesvos had left me very much on the giving side, rarely questioning my own well-being. Yet Beni wasn't asking for any material help, or someone to hold him by the hand and guide him. On the contrary he was looking into my life and what made it what it was. He was looking into my soul; seeking for a person to join him in his asylum-seeking journey and never let go; to grow with him and bear fruit together as one. And I assume this was why he wanted to get to know my mindset. Because he wanted to reach it, understand it and somehow match it. And in all honesty, and as hasty as it sounded, I desired nothing more than to stand by him, and consequently, his journey. Beni's persistence, his pure being and his dire need to make his journey a success impelled me. And the more he opened up to me, the more comfortable I felt with his proximity.

"Sure, it's a nice day," I replied without thinking. "Let's go to the old town and have some coffee."

By coincidence I parked behind Nicosia's municipal market where we had met the night before.

"I recognise this place," said Beni as he looked at the run-down colonial houses that dotted the old town. As we walked through the same pedestrian streets we had discovered to go and get cigarettes, we talked about the division of the capital. He asked if I had Turkish Cypriot friends on the other side of the divide, he ambitiously contemplated the island finding peace one day as though he was making an allegory of his own country. I almost believed that in his mind the French Cameroon side represented the Greek Cypriot side, and the English Cameroon side the Turkish Cypriot one. I was surprised at how easily I referred to Cyprus as my country; my cultural identity so much belonged to this island. Belgium lay deep in my heart but Cyprus was my soul.

We naturally turned to talking politics; how our two countries felt about their colonial history and how religion and nationalism played a role in all of this.

Once settled at the coffee shop, it took some time for us to feel at ease with each other. We were all alone on the terrace. We were sitting face-to-face, small round tables scattered around us. A wall filled with graffiti and half hanging posters of alternative happenings of the capital dressed our surroundings. A cat sat on a chair beside us, soaking up the sunrays that were slowly vanishing as the afternoon descended upon us.

For some time Beni spoke fondly about his mom and stared out into the sky as he told me that he may never see her again. That his decision to leave Cameroon was a very conscious one, but one that ultimately pained him deep in his heart. Saying adieu to a parent is impossible to understand.

"But how did you leave Cameroon? Did you come through Libya or Turkey?" I asked, cringing at the thought of what his journey had potentially involved. I was aware that many Africans came to Cyprus through Libya, leaving its shores through life-threatening boat journeys into Italy and then somehow into Europe. Or, they opted to go to Turkey where they either eventually crossed to Greece by boat; I had met so many of them who had taken that route in Lesvos, or, crossed over to northern Cyprus and eventually made their way into the south of the island, into Europe.

"No. I drove out of Cameroon by car and flew out of Gambia to Turkey and then took a flight to Ercan airport, in the Turkish-occupied areas," he said returning to the present. Our present.

"But, what? You came on a student visa? How did you leave Gambia?"

"I didn't leave Gambia alone. I don't know if we were travelling on a visa or something but there were four of us and this guy that had promised a better life to all of us."

"Like an agent. A smuggler?" I interrupted.

"Yes. Probably more of a smuggler. I paid him a lot of money. Well, my parents paid him a lot of money. He met us at the airport in Gambia, he travelled with us to Turkey and then to Cyprus and took all our papers, our passports and he held onto our air tickets. But the thing is that I didn't know I was coming to Cyprus. I thought that I was going to Germany. My brother lives in Germany."

I could feel he was about to delve into a detailed recollection of the journey that had led him to my realms. Ready or not, I took a discreet, deep breath.

"But how did you cross to the Greek Cypriot side?" The dividing line between the Greek and Turkish Cypriot sides provided a gateway into Europe, and in many cases it wasn't too much of a struggle to get smuggled into the Greek Cypriot side. In many ways it may be one of the cheapest routes to follow. It cost 300 euros per person as opposed to the thousands demanded to cross from Turkey to Greece by boat for example. In Cyprus, some chose to cross the border in the boot of a car, others just walked through the buffer zone and many just handed themselves over to the Greek Cypriot authorities or the UN which controls the area. But I was way ahead of myself.

"When we arrived at Ercan airport, the smuggler told me that we had a couple of hours' wait before we boarded our plane to Germany and that I had to deliver a rucksack to a certain address in Nicosia before we left. That if I didn't, he wouldn't allow me to travel any further. I didn't want to do this. I didn't understand what was going on. He told me that he was going to go and rest in a hotel for a couple of hours, that he would drop me off at the address in question in the meantime. I resisted but eventually I knew I had no option. He was still holding onto all my papers."

He paused often while he spoke and I remained silent at every stop. I wanted to give him the time and space he needed to talk. I didn't want to interrupt his thoughts. I shuffled from side to side on my chair in an attempt to endure his story. His eyes filled with tears and every now and then he would look at me straight in the eyes, pause and smile in contemplation. I'm not sure if he was looking for a reaction or just an understanding that I was following his tracks. My resistance to making any kind of sound grew.

"When he dropped me off at the address by taxi, he told me that he would pick me up from the same place in a couple of hours' time. He gave me a name and told me that all I had to do was give the rucksack he handed me to the man in question, in the apartment that stood above us."

I tried to imagine the state of mind he was in at the time. He had never left his home country. He was brought up on his father's farm where they produced palm oil. He had studied in an all boys' boarding school for the final years of his high school. He had already told me the story about how, due to the civil war in Cameroon and the constant power cuts, he and his father had fabricated a mill in the back of an old car that functioned on the car engine. He drove around the palm plantations in order to mill the palms in what sounded like hectares of land solely filled with palm trees, an exotic vision in my eyes; and now here he was in a country he didn't even know existed, tending to another person's mission.

"So naïve," I thought to myself.

"But didn't you realise that there was something dodgy about this man? I mean, how did you trust him in the first place?" I shook my head from side to side in despair.

"Yes, I believed him. My parents believed him. He was very convincing. This was my only way out, I was going to go and find my brother and build a better life for myself. There is nothing for me in Cameroon. We are so oppressed there. And to be honest, all my parents wanted for me was to work on their farm. I want to study law but I know that I can never practice law in Cameroon. It's so corrupt. I have dreams. I mean I want a simple life, nothing special, but not in Cameroon."

I nodded over and over again holding my coffee cup between the tips of my fingers. In contemplation I powered on through his story, or rather, Beni powered on through *his* story.

"So then what happened?" I continued.

"When I walked into the apartment, the man asked me to open the rucksack. I didn't want to. And I told him this. I told him that I had just come to deliver the rucksack, that it wasn't my job to open it. That he must open it himself. Another man standing behind me threatened to hit me. He was a big man. And I was scared. I didn't know what was going to happen if I didn't obey his instructions, so I opened the rucksack and found a plastic bag in it. I knew something was wrong. And I was stuck."

The atmosphere was heavy. No sunlight could have alleviated the darkness of his words.

"Where was this apartment?" I asked, which was a silly question; of course he didn't know where it was. But he surprised me. And brought me back to reality.

"I told you, I was in Nicosia but on the Turkish Cypriot side."

My hometown had a harsh political reality that was a defining point for anyone living in its periphery.

Regardless, I braced myself for what I was about to hear. For sure, he survived the consequences but I was concerned about the imprint it had left on his soul.

"Did these guys hurt you?" I said shyly, looking at him straight in the eyes.

"When I opened the rucksack and pulled out a tightly sealed plastic bag, he asked me to open it and taste what was in it. I froze. I've never done drugs in my life and I've never wanted to do drugs, ever. It's never been part of my reality. I don't trust myself, I don't think my mind could handle it."

His purity imposed a naivety that perhaps came hand in hand with the restrictions of his existence; living in a palm tree farm, outside of the city for his entire life. Perhaps I was biased but I assumed he had never gone beyond his comfort zone up until he decided to board that plane. The vulnerability he portrayed was as familiar as a child's, yet seeing a person in his early thirties risk his life in such innocence created an ambiguity in his being and fear for his future. I felt that I could believe every single word that came out of his mouth, that there was no hidden agenda, and if he was adamant about getting to know my mindset it was because he equally believed every single word that came out of mine. Instinctively I knew that this was rare.

"I really didn't want to taste whatever was in that bag. I refused. I told the man that I wouldn't do it. And then I woke up lying on the ground in a deserted street surrounded by abandoned houses. My head hurt, but I didn't have any other marks on my body. I had no idea where I was and I had nothing on me. No papers. No money. Nothing. All I had was my cell phone. I was lost. I had no one to call. I couldn't understand what was happening to me."

"But do you have your papers on you today?" I couldn't help myself thinking about the present. He was a legal citizen of Cameroon and to me that's all he could hold on to. I had already begun to think that he didn't belong in Cyprus. He belonged with his family and the nurturing that they only could provide him with.

"I had copies of all my documents on my email. I have everything, I just have to get official hard copies of them," he paused as though it clicked in his head that he had to take care of this, as though I was his mother bickering about something he had every intention of doing but never did.

"I need to go to the Cameroonian Consulate," he concluded.

"But I don't understand how you got to the Greek side," I continued, concerned.

"As I walked around trying to figure out where I was, I met a man in a taxi. He was the one who told me that I was in north Nicosia. That's when I realised that I was in Cyprus. I didn't know much about Cyprus. I didn't even know that the island was divided in two; that Nicosia was cut in half. He's the one who told me that the best thing for me to do was to go to the Greek Cypriot side and seek help. That that would be the place where I could find my way, somehow."

"So he drove you to the south?" I interjected wondering how he had managed to cross the border.

"No, no. He gave me water and drove me to this place where we could see the border from afar. And he told me to walk straight ahead, find someone, anyone and tell them what had happened. That I should apply for asylum there. He dropped me off and left."

Beni looked at the ground. We sat in silence for a long time. I looked at the people that had now gathered around us, enjoying each other's company, sipping coffee, going about their daily lives. Everybody else's life seemed so much easier.

"And so you're waiting for your interview with the asylum services or you've already had an interview? I asked this question thinking that any other question wouldn't do; practicalities were easier to address. Keeping to the facts seemed less painful than delving into how he felt now that he was 'safe' in a country he put so much hope in but which I feared wouldn't meet his expectations.

"I'm waiting for an interview. I've been waiting for almost a month. I don't know when they will call me. There's no indication of time, and anyway they've lost my papers..." he answered, still looking at the ground.

"From what I've heard it can take up to six months to get an interview," I replied bluntly. Beni nodded his head once more. I felt despair although I knew it was nothing compared to the way he felt.

"And, as a political asylum seeker it's important you have proof of what you've fled from. The hardships perhaps that you saw there. Be ready to tell them as much as you can," I added, drinking up my glass of water.

"But do you think they will help me? If I told them the truth about how it really is to live in Cameroon right now?" he continued.

"Well, I'm not the person who can answer that. I assume it depends on why you left. I mean, you're applying for asylum based on what? The political turmoil back home?"

As I prodded for more insight I shifted in my seat once more for I also knew that I couldn't judge anyone for seeking a better or should I say other life in another country, for whatever reason. After all I was a migrant in Cyprus myself. But I also faced the reality that no country would ever take everyone in, that there were rules and boundaries, that people on the move nowadays dealt with very different challenges from what I had to go through two decades ago. In this sense I just hoped he had a valid enough reason to build his case.

"One day I'll tell you what it's like to live within the realms of a civil war and the reason why I left... Being from the English side of Cameroon isn't easy. All the official offices are on the French side and it's difficult or should I say dangerous for us to go there. They insist that we speak French. I understand and speak French of course but how would you feel if they didn't allow you to speak your own language in your own country?"

"Look," I said in a matter-of-fact way. "The truth is that they don't really want you here." I didn't want to sell any lies. I had learnt that lesson back in Lesvos. "There has been a massive influx of migrants in the past couple of years and the government is trying to avoid granting refugee status unless it's clear that your life is under some form of threat, especially if you're not from Syria where there is a war going on." I paused to see if he wanted to speak.

"I needed to hear that from you. I know you won't lie to me and that you have a pretty good understanding of the situation here. At times I wonder whether there's another way around this," said Beni, shuffling on his chair.

"Like what?" I queried.

"I don't know. Maybe one day I will be able to tell you about the life I was leading in Cameroon and what I saw there, how people treated me, what I understood," he repeated. "But now's not the time."

I wasn't sure about what he meant by this. Whether he was referring to a specific incident or whether he was just clutching at straws. But I had a feeling he was keeping things to himself. Self-protection perhaps. Maybe it was just too painful for him to indulge in his past. I left it at that.

That afternoon we parted with an untold understanding that we were together in this, that I was here for anything he needed. That even though he hadn't begun to get to know my life journey, the door was wide open.

Chapter 10

The slap

A couple of weeks later Beni called me from the Nicosia General Hospital. We had seen each other on-off over the past couple of weeks and had become quite close, but I hadn't been in touch for a couple of days. From what he explained over the phone, he had a very high fever and was taken to the general hospital by ambulance after his roommate found him unconscious on the floor in the middle of the night. It was ridiculously cold and although I had given him every single item I had to keep himself warm, I was also aware that it just wasn't enough.

"I don't understand what's going on. They're running all sorts of blood tests for me. I feel better but they won't release me. I'm confused. Everyone's talking to me in Greek. I don't know what's wrong with me. I want to go home," he said urgently on the phone.

When we hung up, I packed the soup I had just prepared for lunch in a Tupperware and went out to find him.

Once at the hospital I found the doctor in charge.

"What are you to him, are you a relative? His girlfriend? I can't tell you anything if you're not related to him," the doctor said as she turned her back to me and began to look through some of the files behind her desk.

I took the plunge. Beni had to understand what was happening to him. "I'm his girlfriend," I interjected, "Can you tell me what's wrong with him?"

"Ah. Nice to meet you," she extended her arm for a handshake. "He's got a constant high fever and we don't know why. We're doing all sorts of tests. From what I understand he's a newcomer to the island. We need to know he's not carrying anything. Malaria. Yellow fever. Typhus. A sexually transmitted disease. Could be anything. We won't let him go until we know." She walked off. Just like that.

Back in Beni's shared hospital room I told him what I had found out. I could tell he was worried but he wouldn't talk. We sat in silence as he sipped on the soup I had brought him. We listened to different conversations going on around the room. The man next to him was preparing to head back home. I assumed Beni wished he was in his shoes.

All of a sudden, Beni broke his silence. "There's something I need to tell you," he murmured as he lay on his side turning his entire body towards me. Before I managed to reply he continued: "I'm not applying for asylum based on political circumstances back home."

"I don't understand," I answered, confused. "We don't

need to talk about this right now, just stay calm," I continued, avoiding what was coming. "What's this got to do with you being in hospital anyway? You need to look after yourself now, the rest can be dealt with later, you..."

"Let me speak," he interrupted. He was anxious.

"I'm bisexual," he blurted out. "I want to seek asylum because I was persecuted for my sexuality back home. I almost got killed. I had to run away," he explained, looking right beside me.

I was speechless. I didn't know what to address first. The fact that he had to be entirely honest with the asylum services? The fact that I was aware that LGBT persons in Cameroon faced legal challenges and that same-sex sexual activity is actually illegal? That they face heavy stigmatisation among the broader population and that if he really experienced this he should tell nothing but the truth? That he should have told the truth to the asylum services from the very beginning? That potentially, he had more of a case telling the truth than by claiming to be a political asylum seeker without evidence? That applying for asylum wasn't a game, that seeking asylum was a procedure that revolved around securing personal safety, that many were taking advantage of the system, that I didn't want him to be one of those people...

But what I really wanted to tell him was that my heart was in knots. Even though I knew that it was normal for someone not to disclose something so personal, I felt that we had spent enough time together for him to do so. We had already shared so much of his journey. I was angry and disappointed. He had lied to me, or chosen to keep one of his deepest truths from me, yet divulged nuances of his being without estimating their impact on my soul. I wanted to tell him that even though I would have never judged him for his sexual preferences, I would have never let myself be vulnerable if I had known that he was bisexual; that I was traditional in my ways; that it was my right to chose whether I would want to indulge emotionally with someone who had inclinations other than mine; that I thoroughly understood his hardships but couldn't let them override my values. That his lying to me potentially implied that every refugee and asylum seeker I had come across had also lied to me. That he shattered the hourglass that encapsulated all the time, heart and energy I had spent on the lives of so many people on the move. That he toppled my resistance against anyone harshly judging refugees' journeys. That I was lost.

After some time I stood up and, in a few words, I said goodbye. When I softened my heart I could easily allow myself to reach out to him and identify with his calling, yet when logic kicked in I was harsh, cold and inapproachable. I had to take a stance on his actions.

You left your sunglasses here, my phone rang as I eventually parked outside my house. *I realise you hate me and that you don't want to see me anymore.*

Hate is a big word Beni, I replied. *I'm keeping my distance. No hard feelings.* I sat on my sofa, dumbfounded.

Days passed. Our contact was brief and painful. A ruptured story extinguished by unrealistic expectations perhaps, on both of our behalves.

I want to go to the asylum services' office. I want to go back to Cameroon. I don't have a place here in Cyprus. I want to go back and join the movement to defeat Paul Biya, the oldest president alive. That was one of the last messages I received from him.

Beni's battles, whether personal or political, were not mine. *If you're not happy in Cyprus, you shouldn't stay,* were my last written words.

He never replied to that text message.

Chapter 11

Coming Home

"I know, I know, it's great, I just think of the ethical perspective from time to time and it really bugs me."

It was early in the morning and I was sitting in a coffee shop in the heart of the old town of Nicosia. Actually, it was the coffee shop where Beni had delicately recounted the story of how he had arrived on the island. Only this time around I was with Marcia. Since I had returned to Cyprus from Lesvos almost three months ago, we hadn't really had time to catch up properly and talk things through like we always loved to do. We spent hours analysing our lives to the bone and I had just finished telling her how my career as a journalist had taken a jolt since I had come back. At times I felt that the word 'refugee' was written on my forehead. That anyone working around the issue of asylum seeking and migration seemed to get in touch with me for some reason or another. I was covering the development of the crisis for the newspaper but not as a full-timer in the newsroom. I had become a freelancer and it was through this independence that I had managed to bring about a prominent human angle to my stories. I did presentations and talks about the understanding that I had formulated over the course of the year. I aimed to raise awareness. I taught creative writing classes to young refugees and tackled their anguish through their writing. I was also involved in art projects that conceptualised migration issues and I was editing an innovative literary magazine whose editorial team and contributors were refugees themselves, a European-funded initiative which aspired to give them a voice but also provide them with an experience of what it meant to be in charge of a publication. I treasured this project, I loved what I was doing and took great pride in shedding a different kind of light on a crisis which was becoming more and more prevalent, especially in Cyprus which had become one of the last gateways into Europe after Turkey had closed its borders. Yet I was troubled with the fact that the migration crisis itself, and on a deeper level the stories of people on the move, had become my breadwinner.

"There are much worse ways to make money, Christine. If I were you I wouldn't even think about that. Would you rather be writing irrelevant stories and spreading the fear-mongering news you always complain about? Seriously, get a grip girl! Look at what you're actually doing." Marcia was always honest with me and had a way of bringing me back to my senses.

"And what about the fact that there are some stories that I just can't write about? Like Beni's story for example. Not that I was initially thinking of writing about him but you know what I mean; there are so many stories out there that just feed in to the overall negative narrative and I just don't want to contribute to that. Like the murder last week. You just know the media's going to blow it out of proportion because it's a third-country national that was the perpetrator. It will reinforce the notion that we shouldn't be 'hosting' them in our 'realms', that all they do is have a negative impact on our society, you know, blah, blah blah. If it had been a Cypriot they would have covered it in such a different light." I was getting annoyed and quite animated as I spoke; however much time passed by I still found it difficult not to get worked up when discussing these issues.

"Look, from the outside looking in, Beni was a personal story, it wasn't a story that you could flaunt on the front page of a newspaper. And in any case, it's not because he's an asylum seeker that the relationship you guys had developed, the way it did. What are you getting in a knot about? I don't get it," said Marcia.

"From all the conversations we've had over the years, you've made me believe that choosing what to write about and how you write about it is your prerogative as a freelancer. Isn't that what you've been after all this time? You can choose what you want to put out there. And you can also choose to take your time in making sense of all the reality you're filtering," she added, leaving me sunk in thought.

In many ways I identified with what Marcia was saying and on some level I had already begun to heal the wounds Lesvos had left on my soul. This meant that I could go beyond merely feeling sorry for the predicament people on the move were faced with. More so than ever, I insisted on their strength being channelled towards their integration in hosting countries and their duty to comply with the new realities they were being faced with: the culture, the language, the system as a whole.

Marcia and I parted for duty called. She was going back to her architectural office and I was heading to an interview with a Syrian family who were facing difficulties in getting medical assistance. The father of the family of six suffered from diabetes and accessing his essential injections was a challenge. The family was applying for asylum and had all the assistance they needed. They were protected by the State, they had an allowance, their children went to school free of charge but in particular it was time sensitivity that they were dealing with, a flaw in the system that didn't allow the father to get the medicine he needed on a regular basis.

I walked into their apartment with a translator who introduced me to the family's four underaged children and their parents. The mother, wrapped in a long tunic and headscarf, occupied herself making us tea whilst the children sat amongst us listening to me talking to their father who was recounting the intricacies of the bureaucracy he had to go through in order to get his medication. I was delighted to hear his two older daughters speak to me in fluent Greek as they explained which local school they went to and what their favourite subject was.

"I have my insulin injections until the end of the month but I don't know whether I will be able to get the next batch in time. Every month we go through this worry, it's exhausting, especially for my wife," said the father looking down at the makeshift carpet and shaking his head. "It's a problem," he added, sitting back on his chair and crossing his legs, his tunic reaching to the top of his ankles. "I can't work due to my illness and we struggle to make ends meet," he continued now sitting up, completely straight with his hands at his side, almost as if vaunting his presence in front of all of us. His wife, who had joined us and had served us very sweet tea in small, flower-printed glasses, just nodded in agreement. I tried to speak to her individually and ask her questions too but she referred me back to her husband all the time.

"But as asylum seekers you're entitled to work in certain sectors, no? I understand that you may not be in a position to work, but does your wife work?" I inquired, looking for a solution more than anything else. I was aware that the sectors the Cyprus State permitted asylum seekers to work in weren't glorious. They included permission to work in agriculture and farming, rubbish collection, car washes; manual work mostly, but as I told everyone, it was better than nothing.

"My wife?" he repeated in surprise. "No, no, in my country women don't work. She needs to stay at home with the children," he stated as a matter of fact. I was offended. As a single working mother I felt his words were critical of me.

"As we speak, I'm a woman at work," I eventually managed to spell out. I had spent a couple of minutes trying to figure out how I was to address this

without sounding too righteous. "I'm sorry to an-
nounce this but in this country this is how things
work. Women work for a living and if it's necessary
for a man to be a stay-at-home dad then so be it.
There's no weakness in that. Women and men have
equal duties, there's no shame in that." I was looking
at him straight in the eyes, leaning forward, conveying some kind of authority.

The translator, a well-composed young woman, must
have felt the tension and opted to intervene. She spoke
to him in Arabic for a while and excluded me from the
conversation. I could tell she was trying to bring the
tone down but I wasn't quite sure if she was justify-
ing my claim or negating it all together. Whatever the
case, I felt my job here was done. I was crossing thin
lines and I wasn't clear on how far I wanted to cross.
I whispered to myself that as a journalist I was there
to gather the facts and bring out the family's reality
through their story and their words; that it wasn't my
job to change their perceptions. At least not with the
journalist's hat I was wearing that morning.

We said our goodbyes with the promise that I would
shed light on the flawed system. That was important.
But I also made sure I conveyed my feelings to the
translator who, as a Syrian refugee herself, could potentially address the gender bias I had just witnessed
with her people; the need for education, the imperative to change a stance that was needed from both
sides of the fence. Locals needed to acknowledge
the plight of refugees but refugees needed to respect

their hosting community and conform with it, in essence. There was no other way forward.

By coincidence, my route home took me past Beni's house. It had been weeks since we had last spoken to each other. And as serendipity goes, I passed Beni riding his bicycle on the side of the road as he ate an apple, holding the steering wheel with one hand. He looked confident and rather free as the spin of his wheels carried him forward. For all this time I had thought that he may have returned to Cameroon somehow, that he wasn't within my realms. I smiled at the idea that he was making a new life for himself here, in Cyprus; that even though he obviously needed to do a lot of soul searching in order to intrinsically grasp his sexuality and feel comfortable with it, he was safe here and wouldn't be threatened by any of his ideals, except the one of lying of course.

Once home I began cooking dinner for Dara and me. It had been a long time since I had felt I belonged somewhere or that the home that I had created with Dara was ultimately the home that I had been seeking for all my life. I had never let myself see that, until that very evening. I tucked her in bed and stroked her hair until she fell asleep. I mused about how fortunate I was for being able to provide for her.

Once sitting in the silence of my living room, I messaged Beni in a bout of forgiveness.

> *"I saw you eating an apple on your bicycle this afternoon. You looked well and perhaps on your way to a good place. I'm happy for you."*

Just as I dozed off, the beep of my phone jolted me awake. I knew it was Beni answering my message and even before I unlocked my phone to glance at his reply, I was certain it would be in the same tone as mine.

> *"Thank you so much for showing me the way. I didn't leave Cyprus after all. I'm applying for asylum as a bisexual, I've found support and I think I have good chances of being approved. I could have never done this without you. I hope your daughter is well and that you remain as strong headed as I remember you. Good night. God bless."*

Photo Credit: Antonis Farmakas

Melissa Hekkers is a Belgian free-lance journalist and author, who has frequently been featured in mainstream news outlets and other publications in Cyprus. Since 2015, Melissa has been teaching creative writing to children and adults. She also focuses on silenced communities in Cyprus: she writes about migrants, both as a reporter and an author; profiles them and teaches them creative and script writing skills through European-funded programmes. In 2007, soon after graduating with a Communications degree, she published her first children's book in both English and Greek, entitled *Crocodile*, which won the Cyprus State Illustration Award. In 2012, she launched her second children's book *Flying across Red Skies* (in English and Greek), using an experimental approach to literature, for which she was nominated for the Cyprus State Literary award. Her third, similarly well-received children's book was *Pupa* (Greek and English), published in 2014 and adapted as a theatre play in 2019. In between her last two books, she published her first free-verse poetry book entitled *Come-forth*. In 2019 she was contributing author to the anthology *Nicosia Beyond Barriers: Voices from a Divided City*, published by Saqi Books, London. *Amir's Blue Elephant* is her first creative non-fiction. She lives and works in Cyprus.